Enjoying Old Parish Churches

Volume 2

By the same author

Essex Fonts and Font Covers
Enjoying Old Parish Churches Volume 1

Enjoying
Old Parish Churches
Volume 2

W.N. Paul F.INST.L.EX.

The Pentland Press
Edinburgh – Cambridge – Durham – USA

First published in 1999 by
The Pentland Press Ltd
1 Hutton Close
South Church
Bishop Auckland
Durham

Typeset by Carnegie Publishing, Carnegie House, Chatsworth Road, Lancaster
Printed and bound by Bookcraft (Bath) Ltd

To my late wife, Pauline, who often patiently waited while I photographed architectural and other features, taking notes, and for allowing me to spend so much time in my study and in research.

Contents

Illustrations

Acknowledgements

I would like to thank my old friend David Philips who accompanied me on many of my visits to parish churches and also to my friends and former students, Ken Feline for his line drawings and Marcus Dain for his line drawings, advice and encouragement.

Architectural Periods

Saxon (pre-Conquest Romanesque)	600–1066
Norman (Romanesque)	1066–1189
Transitional	1145–1189
Early English	1189–1280
Decorated	1280–1377
Perpendicular	1377–1547
Early Tudor	1500–1547
Late Tudor	1547–1603
Jacobean (or early Stuart)	1603–1625
Carolean (or late Stuart)	1625–1649
Hanoverian (William and Mary, Anne, the Georges)	1689–1833
Victorian (Gothic Revival)	1830–1900

Foreword

What a privilege for a crusading church fanatic like me to be invited to compose a Foreword to Volume 2 of this remarkable trilogy, which contains everything that anybody could possibly want to know about our wonderful old churches. How very special these buildings are – their towers, spires and bellcotes gracing our landscapes and townscapes. They fascinate us with living history, delight us with exquisite craftsmanship spanning 1000 or more years and tell us so much about real people from the past. Centuries of prayer and care have made them holy places, capable of bringing us gently to our knees. Every church is a unique sermon in craftsmanship and is the most interesting in the land because it is a 'one-off' – a character well worth getting to know.

Churches first cast their spell upon me when I was four years old. Having been hooked ever since, I try to infect others with their fun and fascination. When people at lectures, slide-shows and excursions have very sensibly asked me to recommend the ideal book about the subject, I have sent them to second-hand bookshops in search of books which have inspired me and which are long out of print.

Not any more, thanks to Norman Paul's painstaking research, which has produced this three-volume oasis of scholarship for the ecclesiologist. As readers of Volume 1 will readily testify, every chapter is a definitive work in itself, containing readable, reasoned and detailed text, laced with illustrations and clear diagrams. Here are the results of a lifetime's love-affair with churches – a kaleidoscope of material which will not only enlighten and motivate the beginner but will also provide much to stimulate the expert.

In this volume we discover many features inside our churches with specific purposes and uses. Although functional, rather than ornamental, these are often masterpieces of craftsmanship and design, because nothing but the best was fit for the House of God. Here we are told of the painstaking methods by which the massive stone mensa-slab (just imagine its weight!) of a mediaeval altar was set apart for its sacred purpose, the pew accommodation for the 18th century squire's churchgoing dogs and even the development of church lighting over the centuries. Every chapter is brimming with examples of the features described.

The author is not only an authority on old churches, but he also loves them, uses them and is part of the life which takes place in them. These buildings rightly provide beauty and inspiration for people of all faiths or of none, but Norman Paul (together with all Christians) naturally looks upon each one of them as 'Home'.

The first word of the title says everything about this book, also about the thrill of churches and the Faith that they proclaim. With all my heart I affirm the 'enjoyment' which these pages generate – and we can enjoy churches so much better if we know what to look for and understand what we see!

Roy Tricker,
(The Churches Conservation
Trust's Field Officer in
South-East England).

Introduction

The Invitation
(sometimes found on old church doors)

Enter this door
As if the floor
Within were gold,
And every wall
Of jewels all
Of wealth untold;
As if a choir
In robes of fire
Were singing here.
Nor shout, nor rush,
But hush ...
for God is here.

(Anonymous)

We, in this country, are immensely privileged in possessing a wealth of parish church architecture which is only compared with France and Italy. The majority of these churches are well worth a visit and contain something of interest. Some of the ancient parish churches existing today were originally either Minster, served by a College of Secular Canons or, until the Dissolution of the Monasteries, were Monastic. Only parts of many of these churches have survived with additional portions having been added in later periods. Our churches not only provide us with an occasion to study church architecture but also unparalleled opportunity for a minority to study the liturgical furnishings which remain in the church from various periods as well as the symbolic significance at the time of their construction.

Much of the high-quality work of the Anglo-Saxon artists and craftsmen was lost when the Normans rebuilt the cathedral and abbey churches and later parish churches, replacing the Saxon work with what they considered to be bigger and better. There are still, however, small amounts of surviving ivories,

I

stone-carvings and manuscripts to enable us to see the high-quality work of the Anglo-Saxons.

With the coming of the Normans the scale of building increased, as did their prosperity and new styles and techniques were imported into the country from the Continent.

Between the Norman period and the Reformation there were many changes in the liturgical requirements as well as the appreciation of beauty and fashion. No complete medieval church interior survives. The Reformation brought with it a spate of destruction and within the space of seventeen years from 1536 all the monasteries were dissolved, churches pillaged, shrines robbed and chantries dissolved. Almost all images were destroyed or decapitated, particular attention being given to the great rood. Altars were thrown out, plate melted down, Easter Sepulchres, fonts and tombs were destroyed and stained glass smashed.

Prior to the Reformation in the sixteenth century the principal focus of the medieval liturgy was the Mass conducted in the chancel, enclosed by the great wooden screen with its rood, in front of the congregation.

Henry VIII had by the Act of Supremacy of 1534 been declared 'Head of the Church in England' following his divorce and remarriage to Anne Boleyn. All these upheavals and developments had a devastating impact on much of the furnishings in churches. Between 1536 and 1553 all the monasteries were dissolved and their churches pillaged. Many of these furnishings associated with traditional devotions such as chantries, images, altars and religious statues, stained glass, paintings, plate and especially the great rood were removed, destroyed or mutilated.

There was far less preaching during Queen Elizabeth's long reign when the Government was nervous as to the rival sinister influences of Rome and Geneva and the clergy were prohibited from preaching, except under licence and could only read a homily to the congregation. The pulpit was profaned and used for political ends of the worst type. For example, William Parry who had been a government spy, was executed for high treason and an alleged attempt to assassinate the Queen. An order of prayer and thanksgiving was issued for the preservation of her life. This order contained an extract from Parry's 'voluntary confession' written to the Queen from the Tower and the minister was commanded at the end of his sermon or homily, on the following Sunday, to read this confession with the statement that he was 'animated thereto by the Pope and his Cardinals'. It is to the discredit of Lord Burghley and the rest of Elizabeth's Council that they caused this 'confession', under the guise of religion, to be read from every pulpit in the land when they were well aware that Parry had retracted this confession on his trial asserting that it was entirely untrue and had been extorted by threats and bribes.

Following the Reformation the emphasis changed from the sacraments to the spoken word, readings from the scriptures and sermons and an Order of Edward VI provided that a pulpit was to be provided in every church; this was ineffective. But when, on the accession of James I in 1603, a similar canon was issued the trickle of new pulpits became a flood and preaching enjoyed a remarkable vogue when passions ran high and when the English language reached its apogee. Later in the century Archbishop Laud and his supporters endeavoured to bring back something of the old character of parish churches, such as reinstating chancel screens, altars at the east end and communion rails, but they were not universally successful.

During the Civil War and the Commonwealth period further damage was carried out to church furnishings by William Dowsing and his gang of iconoclasts and the Puritans who were wholly estranged from the Church. Freedom of speech was restricted and few pulpits were made, although by this time there must have been few churches in need of one. Under the Georgians in the eighteenth century the church furnishings were in conformity with the auditory character of the Protestant liturgy. There was an increase in comfort and box pews were installed as a protection against draughts, and upholstery and heating stoves gave the churches a temporal atmosphere.

The seventeenth century saw the introduction of the two-decker pulpit and in the eighteenth century the three-decker with canopy and standard comprising the pulpit, lectern and clerk's desk. In the early part of the century hatchments were introduced from the Low Countries and when one is able to read them much information may be gleaned about the deceased and the family.

The rich carving to be found in our churches deserves attention and study, especially stone capitals, door arches, corbels, gargoyles and bosses, both stone and wooden. Magnificent carving in wood may also be seen on bench-ends and stalls with their misericords.

During the nineteenth century there was much change, mainly as the result of the Oxford Movement, which led to churches being built in the medieval layout and character of the thirteenth and fourteenth centuries but at the same time new fittings were introduced. Churches, more than any other buildings, are an expression and container of English history from Saxon times to the present day. Where else would be found such treasure houses of sculpture, wood carving, painting, furnishings, stained glass, silver plate and books, most of which are still in their original architectural settings and used with affection and not as museum pieces?

This second volume of the three-volume book, not only gives a general historical background but a good selection of church furnishings and treasures following on from Volume 1. Volume 3 will continue this theme thus making

the three volumes a comprehensive work on historic churches and helping to
bring a greater understanding and love of these sacraments of stone, brick or
rubble.

Piscina

The Latin word *piscina* means 'fish pond' from the Latin *pisces* – 'fish', but in the middle ages the term piscina came to be applied to a shallow saucer-like basin in a niche in the wall on the south side of the sanctuary. The basin had a hole in the bottom and a drain leading to consecrated ground through the wall and floor. It was very necessary that any water which had been blessed or had been in contact with anything consecrated should be returned to earth. The presence of a piscina is usually evidence that nearby there was originally an altar but this does not mean that every altar had a piscina. Where there was an altar and no piscina it must be supposed that the ablutions would have been carried in a basin to the nearest piscina or emptied onto the earth in the churchyard. In the ruins of some English churches, mainly

FOUNTAINS ABBEY, NORTH YORKSHIRE.
Floor piscinas in the Chapel of the Nine Altars.

BARNSTON, ESSEX.
Early double piscina with intersected round arches. Shafts have stiff-leaf capitals.

thirteenth-century, piscinas or drains have been found in the floor near the altars, as for example, at Little Casterton, Leicestershire; Fountains; Rievaulx and Furness Abbeys; Kirkham Priory and Langdon, Kent. It is probably that such floor drains were also common in early parish churches but later disappeared due to repavings. These floor piscinas could have been used not only to receive the rinsings of both hands and vessels but also to receive a little of the contents of the altar cruets before their use in order to remove any dust or other impurity. An unusual combination is to be found at Barton Bendish, Norfolk (St Andrew) where there is a single piscina of the fourteenth century above a double floor piscina which may be earlier. There was a curious custom about the construction of the English piscinas. Until about the middle of the thirteenth century the piscina was usually a single drain and then Pope Innocent IV ordered the washing of the priests's hands before the Mass, deeming it unseemly that these washings should take place in the same basin and so he ordered that there should be two piscinas within the same niche. From that time until the early years of the fourteenth century the piscina was generally double. The double piscina provided one drain to receive the rinsings from the hands and the other from the chalice.

During this period various ablutions took place. In the 1679 edition of his constitution entitled *In Celebratione*, William Lyndwood, fifteenth-century bishop and Chief English bishop and canonist, explains that the washing of the chalice or chalice and paten must be after the Mass was over and so during the period there were three sets of washings or ablutions. Firstly, at the altar during the Mass there was the rinsing of the chalice and of the priest's fingers with wine, these rinsings being swallowed by the priest. Secondly, when the priest left the altar his hands were washed with water which took place at the piscina. Thirdly, after the Mass the chalice or chalice and paten were again washed, which also took place at the piscina. For the two purposes, the vessels and the hands, a double piscina was considered desirable and was, in fact, provided. At East Brent, Somerset and Rothwell, Northamptonshire, to give but two examples, there are triple piscinas which show that there was a rigid rule about the ceremonial of the ablutions.

Early in the fifteenth century there was a reversion to the single piscina due to the low Mass becoming popular which influenced the high Mass tending to abbreviate and simplify it. By 1422 it would seem that the priest no longer left the altar to wash his hands at a piscina, water being poured over his fingers at the altar and then conveyed to a piscina. It would appear to have been thought that it was no longer necessary to provide a separate piscina for this purpose and so the piscina used to receive the water in which the chalice and paten were washed after the Mass, was employed.

Saxon piscinas are rare but there is a triangular-headed piscina at Sompting, Sussex, although it may not be in its original position and has probably been reused. The Saxon piscinas in the ninth and tenth centuries were probably provided as the result of a direction by Pope Leo IV (847–855) that a receptacle was to be provided near the altar for the disposal of the water which had been used in the ablutions of the hands and the holy vessels.

Apart from piscinas set in or against a wall a number of Norman pillar piscinas are to be found, for example, Bardfield Saling (bowl only) and Sandon, Essex; Tollerton, Nottinghamshire and Winchfield, Hampshire. They took the form of a small pillar in the cap of which was carved a basin with a drain passing down the shaft which was sometimes decorated with spiral or zig-zag moulding. Pillar piscinas were still being used in the Transitional period, Norman/Early English and may still be found at, for example, Blakeney, Norfolk. The normal position of a piscina was in the wall to the south of the altar and east of the sedilia, where one existed. However, when an altar was

SOMPTING, SUSSEX.
Saxon gable-headed piscina with interlacing acanthus leaf ornament. The gable-head is probably composed of reused portions from an earlier design.

ST AUSTEL, CORNWALL.
Norman pillar pisciana

GREAT HALLINGBURY, ESSEX. A rare feature of a piscina high up by the side of the chancel arch to serve the rood left.

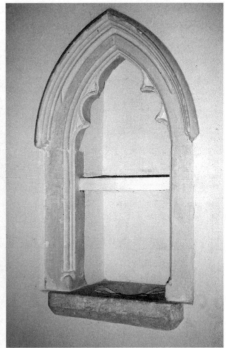

TRUNCH, NORFOLK.
C15 angle piscina.

STOKESBY, NORFOLK.
C14 piscina with shelf.

placed before the east wall of a north aisle or chapel the piscina had sometimes to be placed in the north or east wall. Even when the altar was placed before the east wall of a south aisle the piscina may be found in the east wall, as at Navestock, Essex. Occasionally in an unaisled chancel, the piscina is found in the east wall. Where two separate piscinas are found in the chancel wall it probably indicates that the chancel has been lengthened and that the western piscina is the earlier. An example of this may be found at St John's church, Margate, Kent.

A rare find is a piscina high up near the springing of a chancel arch which probably means that across the arch there was once a rood loft and on the floor of the loft an altar. Examples may be found at Great Hallingbury, Essex and Horningsea, Cambridgeshire.

In the first half of the thirteenth century the fashion came into use in some parts of England of constructing what is generally known as an angle piscina which may be found in the eastern jamb of the south chancel window nearest the altar with a niche opening, usually trefoiled, both to the north and the west often having a shaft between them with moulded capital and base. Good examples, are at Knapton, Norfolk (C14); Blyford, Suffolk (C13) and North Moreton, Berkshire (C14). Also in the thirteenth century, as well as later, a

CASTLE RISING, NORFOLK.
C13 single composition of piscina and sedilia.

stone or wooden shelf was often introduced into the niche over the
piscina drain and was used to place
thereon the cruets and probably the
ciborium or lidded vessel holding the
wafers ready for use at the Mass,
thereby serving the purpose of what
was afterwards termed the credence
table. Where a wooden shelf was used
it has, more than likely disappeared,
but it will still be possible to see the
grooves into which the shelf was fitted
as at St Andrew, Willingale, Essex.

Quite early in the fourteenth century single piscinas returned to fashion
and remained until the Reformation.
They now became incorporated in a
single composition with the sedilia and
in this period there was much enrichment in the form of crocketed and
cusped canopies, trefoiled heads, quatrefoils, mouldings and the ogee arch
(Bardfield Saling, and Little Baddow,
Essex) as well as the popular ball-

MILDENHALL, SUFFOLK.
C14 piscina in external wall for charnel
chapel.

flower decoration. At Cawston, Suffolk, the piscina has an ogee gable with a
wild man and dragon in the spandrels and at Norton Mandeville, Essex, there
is a fourteenth century cusped canopy above a twelfth century pillar piscina
which has been reused. The basins are often large and fluted.

Canopied heads continued into the fifteenth century although some were
straight-headed with vaulting as at Southwold, Suffolk. Generally in this period
the piscina formed part of the design of the sedilia/piscina group.

Sometimes piscina are to be found in the most unlikely places, for example,
on the outside wall of Roughton church, Norfolk and Mildenhall, Suffolk
where they indicate that there is, or was, a charnel chapel.

The fifteenth century showed good design in canopy work and foiled heads
and at Blythburgh and Spexall churches in Suffolk the piscina niches have
cinquefoiled heads. Many piscina niches now have squared heads with various
forms of decoration in the spandrels, for example, a centrepiece within a
quatrefoil set in a circle over an arch having multifoils as at Great Gransden,
Huntingdonshire. Most piscinas of this period are worked in the same design

HEMPSTEAD, NORFOLK.
C15 piscina with foiled head and cruet recess.

SOUTHWOLD, SUFFOLK.
C15 piscina having squared head.

with the sedilia. The exact reverse may be found particularly in the Midlands where frequently there is nothing more ornate than a shallow basin and drain in the sill of a window on the south side of the altar without any niche or canopy over. Examples are at Knipton, Leicestershire; Crich, Derbyshire and Sibthorpe, Nottinghamshire.

Examples from the various periods may be seen:

Norman

Ashe, Hampshire; Bodmin, Cornwall; Crowmarsh Gifford, Oxfordshire; Finchampstead, Berkshire; Fritton, Suffolk; Iford, Sussex; Kilpeck, Hereford and Worcester; Tollerton, Nottinghamshire and West Clandon, Surrey.

Thirteenth Century

Double piscina: Kirksworth, Derbyshire; East Dereham and Carleton Rode, Norfolk; Selby Abbey, North Yorkshire; Cherry Hinton and Trumpington, Cambridgeshire; Barnston and Elsenham, Essex; Adderbury, Oxfordshire.

Single piscina: Baulking, Hampstead Norreys and Uffington, Buckinghamshire;

Kirklington, Oxfordshire; Warmington, Northamptonshire; Gilston and Ippollitts, Hertfordshire; Skelton, Yorkshire; Finchingfield and Chipping Ongar, Essex.

Fourteenth Century

Swavesey, Cambridgeshire; Compton Beauchamp, Fyfield and North Moreton, Berkshire; North Marston, Buckinghamshire; Westhall, Suffolk; Dorchester, Oxfordshire; Great Bedwyn, Wiltshire; Cawston, Norfolk; Stebbing, Little Baddow, Fyfield and Norton Mandeville, Essex; Tollerton, Nottinghamshire; Barton-le-Street and Kirkstall Abbey, Leeds, Yorkshire; Ashe and Winchfield, Hampshire.

Fifteenth Century

Willingale (St Andrew), Essex; Stratford-upon-Avon (Holy Trinity), Warwickshire; Trunch, Norfolk; Widford, Oxfordshire and Amesbury, Wiltshire.

EARLS BARTON, NORTHAMPTONSHIRE.
C12 sedilia graduated in height.

STEBBING, ESSEX.
C13 sedilia with seats on the same level. Note the double piscina.

2

Sedilia

Sedilia is the name given to the seats or recessed canopied stalls usually found near the altar in the south wall of the chancel. The Latin word *sedilia* is the plural of *sedile* which means a seat. Usually there are three seats grouped together, although sometimes less, and which were intended for the use of the priest, deacon and sub-deacon at high Mass which was a lengthy service in medieval times. Occasionally we find four seats together and in a few cases even five.

The earlier examples are generally variously graduated in height with the officiating priest, the celebrant, using the seat at the east end, nearest the high altar, the most honourable position, then the deacon and sub-deacon. The priest celebrated the Mass, the deacon read the Gospel and the sub-deacon read the Epistle. Later, in the fifteenth century, the seats were on the same level and probably marked the time when the assistants at the Mass were priests assisting the celebrant and were used during those portions of the Mass which were being sung by the choir.

The tidal wave of Protestantism swept across sixteenth-century Europe but the Church of Rome did not stand idle and Alessandro Farnese, Pope Paul III, in 1542 summoned to neutral territory at a place called Trent, just north of Italy, a General Council of the Church comprising leading theologians. The Council did not, in fact, assemble until 1545 and owing to various political pressures and interruptions its work was not finished until 1563. Despite the many interruptions and the gathering momentum of the Counter-Reformation the Council during its long and numerous sessions embodied in one coherent code important canons and decrees giving a clear directive to the Roman Church and one which lasted into the twentieth century. The projects of reform aimed at a more precise knowledge of the sacred text, ecclesiology, pastoral education, doctrinal rules and mission, and the Council among the many reforms directed that the celebrant should occupy the central seat of the sedilia. In Mr Francis Bond's book, *The Chancel of English Churches*, he says, 'As late as 1631 a definite statement was made in a Roman Missal published at Antwerp, that the sedilia were to be occupied by the celebrant, deacon and sub-deacon while the choir sings the Kyrie Eleison, Gloria, Excelsis and Credo but that at the Mass the celebrant should sit on the Epistle side of the altar between the deacon and sub-deacon.' Where more than three seats are found the additional seats were used when the bishop was present and was officiating pontifical Mass. Extra accommodation would be needed on these occasions for the bishop's chaplain and others. From the twelfth century onwards a permanent feature of the chancel was the sedilia and in the thirteenth century they became fairly general but the largest number belong to the fourteenth century when the favourite objects on which art and money were lavished were the sedilia, piscina, Easter Sepulchre and spire, just as a century later the popular furnishings were the chancel screen, stalls, benches, roof and porch.

The design of the sedilia varied according to the prosperity of the parish but there are exceptions as in the richly decorated church at Bloxham, Oxfordshire, where there are plain stone benches. In some cases the sedilia are merely plain stone benches, with or without arms to mark the divisions, while others are composed of a stone slab in a canopied recess, an example of which may be seen at Gestingthorpe, Essex. In some parts of the country, particularly in East Anglia, the most inexpensive form of sedilia was obtained by lowering the sill of a window south of the high altar as at Trunch, Norfolk, or in some cases they may be wooden stalls as at Rodmersham, Kent. In the best designs the sedilia and piscina are all part of the one design in one composition

MONYASH, DERBYSHIRE.
C12/13 sedilia with dog-tooth design. Each sedile separated by slender shafts.

STRATFORD-ON-AVON, WARWICKSHIRE.
C15 rich sedilia with nodding arches and a row of angel busts in front of the seats which are on the same level.

where each sedile occupied a central niche with its own arch or richly carved canopy. In the early work of the Norman and Early English periods the tendency was to separate each sedile by slender shafts but in later work they were divided by walls which were frequently pierced with cusped arches.

The design detail of the sedilia naturally followed that of the constructional members of the church such as the arcades and so in the twelfth century the sedilia had semicircular arches, scalloped capitals and chevrons, nailhead or other Norman decoration. There are few examples of Norman sedilia but some may be seen at Earls Barton, Northamptonshire; Shrewsbury, Shropshire and at Castle Hedingham, Essex.

In districts where there was a plentiful supply of stone much skill and delicacy of treatment was expended in the enrichment of canopy work and frequently the piscina was included with the sedilia and formed part of the composition. During the first half of the thirteenth century the arches were delicately moulded (Chedzoy, Somerset and Coulsdon, Surrey) and towards the end of the century crockets appear and a pedimental gable was common remaining in many designs to the first quarter of the fourteenth century (Easthorpe, Essex).

WINCHCOMBE, GLOUCESTERSHIRE. C15 sedilia. Seats on same level. Separated by image niches and having crocketed canopies.

MALDON, ESSEX. C14 sedilia with fine cusping. Graduated seating.

In the second half of the fourteenth century through to the end of the third quarter there were many rich and elaborate examples incorporating much use of the ogee arch and cusping as at Fakenham, Norfolk; Shalford, Essex and Swavesey, Cambs. By the middle of the fourteenth century churches had been plentifully equipped with piscina and sedilia and perhaps the best examples are from this period (Ludlow, Shropshire; Tideswell, Derby).

The fifteenth century produced some fine sedilia of a varied nature, some having shallow canopies as at Kirk Hallam, Derbyshire, while at Rotherham, Yorkshire, the dividing walls are wide and are pierced and cusped. Yet again some have very fine canopies running over a table bench, the seats of which are not divided, a good example being at Southwold, Suffolk. Where the sanctuary had an aisle or chapel to the south the sedilia could not be built into the wall and therefore stood detached necessitating ornamentation at the back as well as the front as at Tewkesbury Abbey, Gloucestershire and Crediton, Devon.

As the medieval services were lengthy two of the priests during the singing of the Kyrie Eleisan, Credo etc. might play a game called Nine Men Morris. This game was played on three squares, one within the other, scratched on the stone seat. Each corner was marked and the three squares were joined by

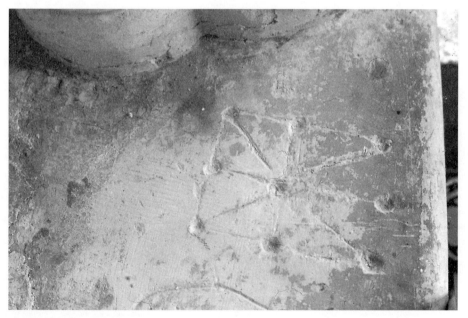

GREAT SAMPFORD, ESSEX.
Small edition of Nine Men Morris scratched on one of the stone seats which run along the sides of the chancel.

a line on each side with each point of intersection being marked. The game was played with counters (men) each player having nine men placing them alternately on the vacant dots. When a line of three men had been formed the player had made a mill. As soon as all the counters had been placed on the board either player could move his pieces alternately along the lines into any adjoining space in an endeavour to make further mills and reduce his opponent's pieces. As soon as a player had made a mill he was entitled to remove one of his opponent's pieces provided it was not already part of a mill. Jumping over places was not allowed. The player who is reduced to two counters or is in such a position as to be unable to move any of his pieces has lost the game. The design has been found by archaeologists in many parts of the world and is said to date to at least the Bronze Age *circa* 1800–550 BC. Boards may be found in other parts of the church, for example, on the sill of a window as at Finchingfield, Essex.

3

Aumbries

An aumbry is a cupboard in the wall near the altar, generally a square or rectangular recess having a wooden door, if it still exists, of an ornamental character as at Minster, Kent, where the aumbry retains its original door with linenfold pattern. Occasionally the doors were strengthened with iron scroll work. In a few cases the recess would have a moulded head, for example, lancet, ogee or trefoil head but the recess would still be square or rectangular. At Salisbury Cathedral there are two aumbries, one of which is triangular headed and the other trefoil headed within a pointed moulded arch. (Sefton, Merseyside, Ogee; Salisbury Cathedral, Wiltshire, Trefoil; Trunch, Norfolk, Lancet.)

Very few of the early churches had sacristies and the priest vested at the altar, his vestments being stored away in the church chest and the vessels used at the altar and font being kept in the aumbry or aumbries and so it would appear that the chest and aumbry were the forerunner of the later vestry. At Durham it was specified that one of the aumbries was to be used 'to set the chalices, the basons and the crewetts ... with locks and keys'.

Aumbries were also used for other purposes such as a receptacle for reliquaries, deeds and indentures and valuable documents. The inside of the aumbry frequently contained a stone or wooden shelf and where the wooden shelf has disappeared the grooves which formerly supported it may still be seen as at Rattlesden, Suffolk. Where the original door has disappeared the pivots of the hinges may still be found or holes showing where they had been fixed. As the south side of the chancel usually contained the piscina and credence, sedilia and the priest's doorway the normal position for the aumbry was on the north side. Where there was an altar at the east end of a south aisle the appropriate aumbry would have to be on the south wall of the aisle. Wherever there was an altar, both piscina and aumbry were placed in the most convenient position that could be found. Occasionally two or more aumbries may be found near the high altar and occasionally one may be found in the east wall of the chancel. It has been said that where there is an eastern aumbry it was probably used for the Reservation of the Holy Sacrament and was known as the Sacrament House. In England the Blessed Sacrament was reserved so that it might be

WITNEY,
OXFORDSHIRE.
C13/14 aumbry
showing rebate
for doors and
remains of hinges.

GREAT
WALSINGHAM,
NORFOLK.
C14 aumbry with
original door.

ITCHINGFIELD, SUSSEX. Norman
aumbry with semi-circular arch.
Modern door.

Suspended dove pyx and canopy.
Madonna and Child finial.

taken to the sick and dying. Reference to this is shown by the many entries
to bell, book and candle in churchwardens' accounts. The position for the
storage of the Reserved Sacrament, however, varied. The normal method was
to reserve it in a pyx suspended in front of and above the altar. This pyx was
a box of wood, ivory or metal covered with some costly fabric. A crane or
pulley was arranged over the altar to enable the pyx, which was suspended by
a chain or cord attached to a ring at the top, to be raised or lowered. There
are few pyx remaining but it may be possible to see in the roof the pulley
which was used. A further method was to enclose it in a small coffer which
was placed on the altar. At St Stephen, Coleman Street, London, the records
show that in 1466 there is mention of 'one coffer for to keep the Sacrament
on the high altar'. Some were in the form of a tower and occasionally made
of gold. It would seem, therefore, that the method used for the Reservation
of the Sacrament was not always uniform. Later, built upon or on part of the
altar was a substantial 'tabernacle' which contained a small cupboard having a
lock and key and which today may be seen on most Roman Catholic altars.
There was a third method which was to Reserve the Sacrament in a cupboard

or aumbry which was constructed in the wall and provided with a door, lock and key. This method is still used in some churches.

The Reserved Sacrament today is denoted by a small lighted oil lamp suspended in front of the altar. This practice is not new as it was also practised in the Middle Ages.

Aumbries with original doors may be seen at: Aston and Great Walsingham, Norfolk; Kingsmead, Northamptonshire; Barrington, Cambridgeshire; Sefton, Lancashire; Chaddesden, Derbyshire; Minster, Kent and Salisbury Cathedral, Wiltshire.

A tabernacle may be seen at Warkleigh, Devon, a pyx cover at Dennington, Suffolk and a pulley socket at West Grinstead, Sussex. The pyx was usually veiled out of reverence and a medieval veil survives at Hessett, Suffolk.

4

Altars, Altar Rails, Altar Coverings and Reredoses

An altar has been an essential part of the furniture of a church since earliest times and was the central object without which the performance of worship was impossible. The altar was no accessory, it was the church, not the altar, which was the accessory. The church was primarily the shelter for the altar.

In England, in pre-Norman times the altar was frequently called 'Christ's Board' or 'God's Board' and this continued for two or three centuries after the Conquest. The pagan convert found the altar familiar as Roman or Greek temples had altars. Roman altars may still be found in museums or used as

CHICKNEY, ESSEX.
C13 mensa having five consecration crosses and mounted on a modern base.

milestones and even as fonts (Chollerton, Northumberland) or as a holy water stoup at Auckland, Durham.

Wooden altars were in general use for the first four or five centuries being common in Anglo-Saxon England and lingering on in England till the end of the eleventh century, and were even to be found down to the Reformation as can be proved from old inventories and wills. In 1432 John Ravensthorpe who was a priest of the chapel of St Martin, Aldwark, North Yorkshire, left a vestment to the wooden altar of that chapel.

The wooden Anglo-Saxon altars were ordered to be destroyed in his diocese by St Wulstan, Bishop of Worcester (1062–1095) and following the Conquest the council of Winchester under Lanfranc and the Papal Legate issued an edict in 1076 against their use and ordered that altars should be made of stone. The stone altars were mostly copies of wooden altars and were each composed of a large rectangular slab of freestone or marble, bevelled on the under surface, marked with five crosses and supported by four columns or legs or a sub-structure of stone. The slab was known as a 'Mensa' from the Latin for 'table'. The practice of having five consecration crosses, one in the centre of the slab and one in each corner, was normal from the twelfth century. The five crosses are said to be in memory of the five wounds of Christ but the crosses really mark the places where the bishop touched the altar with the holy oil during the act of consecration as he did the consecration crosses on the church walls when the church was consecrated. On the other hand he may well have touched the altar at five points with symbolic intent. There are examples where there are either less or more crosses, e.g. at Cotes-by-Stow, Lincolnshire there are six crosses on the mensa and at Broughton Castle chapel, Northamptonshire there are nine crosses.

An article written in the *Antiquary* by a Father Morris stated that in the consecration of altars a small fire was made in each of the incised crosses. Five pieces of incense were put on the crosses and on the pieces of incense a cross was made of thin taper wax which was lighted at the four ends. When the fire was burnt out the ashes were scraped away with a wooden spatula but as the cross was incised the scraping was only flush with the surface, so it retained the melted incense which had run into it. It would seem that the crosses were cut in the mensa whether the ceremony of formal consecration was carried out or not, although no altar could be used for celebration without consecration.

Many of the side altars were not consecrated owing to the difficulties of travelling which prevented the bishop attending to consecrate all the altars which were set up in his diocese, particularly when the chantry chapels became popular. This situation was overcome by the bishop consecrating numerous super-altars which were much smaller, and lighter altar stones on which it was

BINHAM PROIRY,
NORFOLK.
Altar Consecration Cross.

Reliquary, late C12. Figures of twelve apostles. Limoges painted enamel, British Museum.

lawful to celebrate Mass and which could be placed on top of the unconsecrated mensa. They were used on journeys, in camps and in the visitation of the sick and it was also necessary to use them when the altar was made of wood following the Council of Winchester's edict of 1076. There is an example in Beckermet church, Cumbria, where the super-altar is made of red sandstone and measures ten inches by seven and a half inches and is three-quarters of an inch thick and has five consecration crosses.

Medieval altars varied in size according to the building and the position they occupied. Some altar slabs belonging to minor altars are approximately three to four feet in length while high altar slabs may measure well over thirteen feet with a thickness of some six to eight inches, as at Tewkesbury Abbey. In accordance with the direction of Pope Innocent III the slab had to be one unbroken piece of stone. D. Rock in his book, *Church of our Fathers* (1905), states that the whole stone symbolises 'the unbrokenness of the Church and the oneness of her belief'. It will be apparent, therefore, that the weight of such a stone would be considerable, something in the region of three-quarters of a ton or more.

Many altar slabs have been found and reinstated since the middle of the last century and at Borley church, Essex a medieval slab was recovered in 1943. The slab was set lengthwise in the floor of the nave, about five inches of one end being covered by the chancel step. The rector was of the opinion that as it was so close to the monument to the Waldegrave family it was probably the entrance to the family vault. In 1943 he caused the stone to be partly raised but nothing was found beneath it and it was left in position. Later, a mason from Sudbury noticed certain features which suggested that it was probably a medieval altar slab. In 1946 the rector had the slab taken up and it was found to measure five feet four inches by two feet eleven and a half inches and six inches thick. Three of the lower edges were chamfered to a depth of two and a half inches, the back edge being left square. The wear to which the slab had been subjected over centuries probably accounted for the absence of definite remains of the usual five consecration crosses although slight traces of a cross could be discerned in the lower right-hand corner. The date cannot be definitely ascertained but the chancel was rebuilt in *c.*1500 and the slab is only six inches less than a third of the width of the chancel, i.e. seventeen and a half feet. The slab was re-erected on four stone supports and a service of rededication was held on 15 June 1947.

Each consecrated altar required a vessel or container called a reliquary accompanied by a descriptive scroll or parchment on which was written the name of the consecrator, the date and a note of any indulgence or grant. The reliquary was sometimes placed in a small cavity called the *confessio* or *sepulchram altaria* which was sealed or closed by the Bishop with a thin stone called *segillum*, the place of the seal. Where there was an altar table the reliquary, which would be a decorative vessel probably with precious stones, would be placed between the legs whether the altar be made of stone or wood. The reliquary probably contained fragments of the body of a saint, for example, bones, hair, fingers or some article, including clothing, which had belonged to the saint.

This practice of placing relics in a *confessio* was widely used between the sixth and ninth centuries when a widespread devotion to relics of the saints became popular, the altar becoming a kind of tomb housing the body of a saint as at St Peter's, Rome. In the tenth century it became general that the enshrined relics should be 'elevated' and placed over altars for public veneration. Up to this time the high altar had stood out as a prominent feature as the stone of sacrifice being kept clear and treated with great respect. Now, however, it began to be cluttered by reliquaries placed either on the table, or where they were large, enshrined behind and above the altar.

The cult of the saints and the invasion of relics was destined to change, gradually, the character, disposition and even the situation of the high altar so that it became necessary to combine the altar with the relic shrine and the table instead of being square and small became rectangular and larger. The reliquary behind and above the altar became larger and larger and more ornate, being the centre of attraction and far outweighing the altar as the most prominent feature of the sanctuary. The ever-growing relic shrine led to the abandonment of the *confessio* and to the disappearance of the civory, a canopy over the altar.

In the eleventh and twelfth centuries an elementary fixed retable or altar-piece made its appearance as a support for the reliquary over the altar. By the end of the fourteenth century the retable which hitherto had been of modest proportions had now become a great structure lending itself to the art of the sculptor and painter. During the century it grew even larger becoming more complicated and flamboyant. These retables either stood on their own foundations or rested on the altar itself and gave the impression that the table of the altar was merely the base for a mass of ornamentation. These huge retables became the dominant feature of the altars of the fifteenth to the eighteenth centuries. The position of the altar was also changed and instead of being fully detached and standing out clearly in the middle of the sanctuary it was moved back against the east wall where it merged into the background and became even more insignificant. The dominant features of high altars of this period were size and over-ornamentation which were in keeping with Renaissance ideas. In addition to over-ornamentation to the altar on great feast days there was ornament in the way of extra candlesticks, reliquaries, church plate etc.

piled on the altar table. To add to all this the gradine, which was a step or shelf, frequently a thin stone slab at the back of the altar slab, made its appearance at the end of the fifteenth century. This shelf was probably used to support a small reredos or in some cases statuettes, as, for example, Clapton-in-Gordano, Somerset, where the gradine contains three hollows in which are holes formerly containing irons which supported statuettes.

It will be remembered from the chapter on aumbries that the Reserved Sacrament was kept in a tabernacle on the altar. At the end of the fifteenth century the tabernacle had become an ordinary feature of the High Altar being sometimes an elaborate structure over-sized and over-ornate while some were just holes in the enormous structure in which they were embedded. This craving for enormous ornate structures resulted in the altar losing its significance so that it was dwarfed out of all recognition and ceased to be the focal point of the church. In a few places, however, the simple dignified altar was preserved and in the seventeenth and eighteenth centuries there was a reaction which led to the restoration in some churches of the Roman type of altar, the simple table containing six tall metal candlesticks with a large metal crucifix in the centre, the whole surmounted by a canopy which symbolised the traditional mark of reverence and honour, emphasising the royal dignity of the altar and covering it and the ministers as they stood before it, as they and it represented Christ.

GREAT MASSINGHAM, NORFOLK.
Elizabethan altar table.

As a result of the Reformation in the sixteenth century the old stone altars were ordered to be overthrown and only a few original stone altars are now standing in English churches, e.g. Arundel, Sussex and Peterchurch, Hereford & Worcester. In the 1550 Act against Superstitious Books and Images, Edward VI, ordered that stone altars be removed and holy tables of wood be installed. There are, however, a number of cases where the old mensa or altar slab still remains either set in the floor like a ledger stone or has been restored to its original use. An example of this may be seen in Chickney church, Essex where the mensa was found under the floor during restoration work in 1858 and re-erected. At Wigborough Green, Sussex, the mensa was used as a chimney breast in a kitchen and later as a seat in the vicarage garden. It is a fine Norman mensa, six feet long and about a foot thick and is said to weigh a ton. It was restored in 1937.

Although wooden altars were in the vast majority, the injunctions of Elizabeth in 1559 did not order the removal of stone altars. The Elizabethan altars were frequently beautifully carved usually with great bulbous legs. The early Jacobean altars also had bulbous legs and were well carved. Some good examples are to be seen at: Evesham, Hereford & Worcester; Dinton, Buckinghamshire; Cheddar, Somerset; Burlescombe, Devon and Ombersley, Hereford & Worcester. Even in the seventeenth century Puritan animosity against the Church was displayed in the furious attack made by the Long Parliament of 1640 when Commissioners were appointed to visit the counties and 'destroy all images, crucifixes, superstitious pictures and altars or holy tables turned altar-wise that yet remained in churches'. In 1643 an Ordnance of the Lords and Commons was issued for the demolition of all altars and tables of stone. Right through the sixteenth and seventeenth centuries orders of various kinds were given to destroy stone altars but it is evident that these orders were not fully carried out.

During the reign of James I, when under the leadership of Archbishop Richard Bancroft, the Church had acquired a greater sense of cohesion, churchmen began to realise that the current method of arranging the communicants and the placing of the altar had certain serious disadvantages. In days when the churches had to serve not only as places of worship but often as schools and parish halls, an altar lying in the middle of the chancel or at the east end of the nave was a tempting thing for anyone to use who happened to want a table. As a rule an altar was quite unprotected and churchwardens found it convenient to sit round it when making up their accounts; children, if they were taught in the church, used it as a writing table; workmen put their clothes and tools on it; animals could easily profane it. No doubt this way of treating altars was due more to thoughtlessness than intentional irreverence.

MENDLESHAM, SUFFOLK.
C17 altar table.

The dissatisfaction felt by so many with what had become the accepted method of positioning the altar and of giving Communion led to the famous controversy on altars which played such a large part in the life of Archbishop Laud and so in the seventeenth century the altar reverted to its usual position at the east end of the church. There are still some, however, who, even today, feel that the holy table should be in the nave and in some churches we can find the altar or holy table in the east end of the nave, for example Ware church, Hertfordshire where the holy table and seats are modern.

It is difficult for us, in the twentieth century, to appreciate just how great were the sweeping changes caused by the Reformation and the impact which such changes made on the people. The traditional furnishings and decorations of the church all smashed and swept away; the alteration in language from Latin to English; a different form of service and changes in attitude. Prior to the Reformation religion was a matter of form and ritual, with particular ceremonies being performed in a certain manner according to a regular calendar of feasts and fasts. The Mass had a majestic symbolism and the other services had a colourful pageantry which formed part of the traditional life of men and women. The annual round of ceremonies at Christmas and Easter and the more sombre ones of Lent and Holy Week, as well as others, all gave form and order to both secular and religious life. In a few years, however, all these were swept away or entirely altered and this traumatic disturbance must have been very great both for individuals who, in the main, had received little or no education, as well as for the community.

In modern times we remember the discussions which took place in 1965 when the Alternative Prayer Book services were allowed, called Series 1, later to be superseded by Services 2 and 3 and finally published as an alternative to the Book of Common Prayer in 1980. The Church was divided, some still wishing to retain the 1662 Prayer Book services and others opting for the new form. This, however, was not be compared with what happened in the sixteenth century when, apart from anything else, beautiful furnishings, plate, stained glass, roods and screens, statues and much else were lost and gone for ever. A way of religious life which had been known and enjoyed by the people for centuries had been swept away.

Altar Rails

From early times it was the custom not only to fence off the chancel from the approach of the laity but also to veil it from their gaze and so there was no need for altar rails, the screen, which every church possessed, at the entrance to the choir, being sufficient.

During the celebration of Mass the laity communicated outside the choir and were rigidly excluded from the chancel, except the king and the nobility of the realm, and so the altar needed no protection beyond the chancel screen. When, however, the reformers pulled down the screens and the Puritans began to drag the altars into the midst of the chancel or the nave, placing them table-wise, it became necessary to provide some new form of protection.

It was during the latter part of the reign of Elizabeth that the use of altar rails began but they did not become general until the days of Archbishop Laud who was Dean of Gloucester Cathedral in 1616, Bishop of London in 1628 and Archbishop of Canterbury in 1633. Whilst Dean of Gloucester Cathedral Laud moved the altar or communion table against the east wall of the sanctuary and put a rail in front of it to symbolise the central place of the Eucharist in Christian worship and to restore the altar to its original position in church buildings. Prior to this the table was, in some cathedrals and royal chapels, placed north and south at the east end of the choir but it was usual at communion to turn the table so as to be east and west and place it in the middle of the choir. Later in 1624, as Archbishop of Canterbury, Laud directed that the holy table should occupy the same position as the ancient altar and that it should be railed in, which was usually done on three sides, and that the table should

THORPE, DERBYSHIRE.
C16 altar rail.

remain in one fixed position at all times against the east wall. Some churches disregarded the direction and railed the table on four sides as at Lyddington, Leicestershire. The placing of these rails so as to enclose the table was a visible assertion of the sanctity of the altar and its mysteries and so the Puritans detested them and many rails were pulled down especially by William Dowsing, the Parliamentary Visitor of Churches during the Civil War, whose function was to enforce an Order for the destruction of monuments of superstition and who took the opportunity to pull down altar rails wherever he found them.

There were still many Puritans, clergy and laity, in the Church of England who opposed Laud's reforming zeal and this opposition came to a head in 1640 when the Convocation of Canterbury and York made the permanent placing of the communion table against the east wall compulsory. Soon afterwards many of the rails were removed and at Sandon, Essex, they were burnt on the village green.

The rails were provided with a gate in the centre and the closeness of the balusters to each other was to prevent dogs from getting into the sanctuary and profaning the altar. The Visitation Articles of the Caroline Divines clearly showed that the communion rail should be, 'Enclosed and ranged about with a rail of joiners and turners work close enough to keep out dogs from going

POLSTEAD, SUFFOLK.
C18 altar rail on three sides.

in'. These Caroline Divines were a group of Cambridge scholars which included such famous names as John Cosin, Thomas Fuller and Nicholas Ferrer. Each in his own way made his own contribution to the life of the Church and gave it the self-confidence and inner-sense which enabled it to rise again after the disasters of the Civil War and Commonwealth. They were concerned in getting back to the early Church before the growth and additions, for example, indulgences, of the Middle Ages which the Reformers had been so anxious to get rid of. Bishop Wren in his Visitation in 1636 said, 'The Rayle be made before the Communion Table reaching crosse from north wall to the south wall neare one yard in hight, so thick with pillars that dogs may not get in'. It is obvious, therefore, that the purpose of these rails was not to provide support for the communicants to lean against when they received Holy Communion as the height of these seventeenth century rails would have made them very inconvenient for the kneeling communicant. It is not to be thought that communion rails were not in use until the time of Laud as they were in use in early post-Reformation days. The altar rails at Flintham, Nottinghamshire are *c.*1600 and at Elton, Nottinghamshire early seventeenth century and clearly before Laud's days. The altar rails of Langley Marsh, Buckinghamshire are dated

1625. Where, however, Puritans held benefices communion rails were not tolerated.

Altar rails of the Laudian period or of the latter part of Charles I's reign still remain *in situ* in some churches but many were destroyed during the 'so called' restorations of the last century. Examples may be seen at Winchfield, Hampshire; Langar, Nottinghamshire; Knipton, Leicestershire; Kingsthorpe, Northamptonshire; Lingwood, Norfolk; Studley, Warwickshire; Hunsdon, Hertfordshire and Lanteglos, Cornwall. A few of the rails which had been placed round three sides of the altar table have survived and examples may be seen at Poynings, West Sussex and Langley, Shropshire.

Most of the rail balusters followed the patterns of the legs of tables and chairs and the balusters of the pulpit or gallery stairs. The simplest form of railing was merely a row of forms but the common type was constructed of balusters having a central bulge (West Stafford, Dorset and Cliffe at Hoo, Kent). A further type is the twisted baluster which was common in staircases and furniture (Great Staughton, Cambridgeshire and St Stephen, Walbrook, London). Usually the twisted baluster belongs to the first half of the eighteenth century but some may be earlier. Later, balusters were discarded in favour of foliated panels of classical type as at Winchester Cathedral which rails are attributed to Grinling Gibbons and St Decuman, Watchet, Somerset, dated 1688.

In 1643 the Commonwealth Parliament passed an Act 'for the utter demolishing, removing and taking away of all monuments of superstition and idolatry' and so it must be assumed that many altar rails were destroyed. It would appear that many churches remained without altar rails till a later period. As late as 1704 Bishop Nicholson found thirty-five unrailed chancels in the diocese of Carlisle (Cox's Churchwardens' Accounts).

CAWSTON, NORFOLK.
C17 Laudian altar rail.

TREDINGTON, WARWICKSHIRE.
Houselling bench.

After the Restoration in 1660 it became more and more the tendency to put up altar rails however now they were no longer erected in the Laudian or Puritan fashion round the holy table but in a single continuous row extending across the chancel to the west of the holy table.

Prior to the introduction of altar rails when chancel screens were the invariable rule of the Church there was no need for altar rails and it was the custom for houselling benches to be used for the infirm or aged communicants. The Saxon word 'husel' means 'eucharist' or 'sacrifice'. A houselling bench was a movable wooden bench which was placed before the aged or infirm communicants and covered with a houselling cloth which was a long towel of linen, or very occasionally a silken sheet, the purpose of which was to prevent crumbs from the Blessed Sacrament falling to the floor. The houselling cloth was also used for other communicants as they knelt to receive the Eucharist and was held before them to catch any particles of the Sacrament which might fall during the administration. Even after altar rails were introduced into churches houselling cloths were frequently spread over them. It is understood that in 1916 houselling cloths were still being used in Wimborne Minster, Dorset and in Brecon Priory, Powys and a houselling bench may still be seen at Tredington, Warwickshire. Many other churches retained the use of the houselling cloth well into the nineteenth century, e.g. Chesterfield, Derbyshire; Sellack, Hereford & Worcester and Swayfield, Lincolnshire. The medieval parish was a community residing in an area defined by the Church and subject to her authority. The members of the community were known as 'housellings' or 'communicants' as they would be called today. They owed the duty of worship in the parish church and as far as their means permitted made contributions towards the church expenses.

For over one thousand years the normal position for receiving the Eucharist was standing and this is still the norm in France and Switzerland. It was only during the thirteenth century that the custom of kneeling came into general use when the elevation of the Host became established and reverence was shown by kneeling with bowed head.

Altar Coverings

Except for the first few centuries altars were covered with a decorated cloth embroidered with emblems and sometimes with jewels over which was placed a linen cloth, usually white, when the altar was used for the celebration of the Eucharist. In the second part of the Middle Ages in the West, when altars came to be placed close to screens and walls, the decorated cloth was abandoned for a frontal, a flat silk cloth which was suspended on the side of the altar which was visible to the congregation. Today, a linen cloth usually covers the top of

AXBRIDGE, SOMERSET.
Altar frontal, 1720.

the altar particularly at the time of the celebration of the Eucharist and there is also a frontal, the colour of which changes according to the seasons of the Church's year. White is used on feasts of our Lord, the Blessed Virgin Mary, Angels and Saints who were not martyrs, Eastertide, Trinity Sunday and All Saints' day; red is used at Whitsun and feasts of martyrs; violet for Advent and Lent, Rogation and Ember days; green is used on Sundays throughout the seasons of Epiphany and Trinity and on weekdays on which no special feast or fast is being kept; black may be used on Good Friday and All Souls' day as well as for funerals and requiems. Today it is usual to strip the altar on Maundy Thursday and Good Friday.

A beautifully decorated, hand-made altar frontal made in 1720 may be seen at Axbridge, Somerset.

Reredoses

It was usual to place behind the altar some special background such as drapery, wall paintings, painted wooden panels or some sort of masonry erection. The earliest English reredoses were mural paintings on the east wall like the thirteenth-century painting at Great Canfield, Essex, the twelfth-century paint-ing at Copford, Essex or the Norman painting on the wall at St Alban's Cathedral. The high altar also had the stained glass of the great east windows as the parochial reredoses in parish churches which probably accounts for the size of many an east window where the sills come down to within three or four feet of the altar table. The space on the wall between window and altar, in the later Middle Ages, was filled in with a structure of wood or stone extending the length of the altar forming a reredos. It was sometimes made of alabaster and whether wood or stone was seldom left without gilt and colour. Reredoses may be divided into those of stone and those composed of wooden panels.

Stone reredoses were either free standing or attached. There are a few fine free-standing examples beautifully sculpted as at Christchurch, Dorset with its figures set in small niches and a large central group representing the tree of Jesse. They usually consist of lofty walls of masonry enriched with tabernacle work and there may be niches containing figures. In the smaller churches the wall itself at the back of the altar was treated as a reredos and was sometimes formed of arcading, panelling or a sculptured table let into the wall. An example of this type may be seen in Chichester Cathedral and another, of the fifteenth century, at Ludlow, Shropshire which still preserves some of its fine original statuary.

There are some fine examples of wooden reredoses with some containing painted panels. In Norwich Cathedral is a fourteenth century reredos with

TIDESWELL, DERBYSHIRE.
C14 stone reredos.

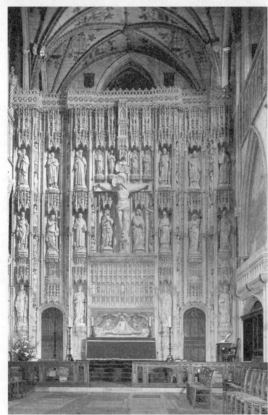

ST ALBANS CATHEDRAL,
HERTFORDSHIRE.
C15 stone reredos with three
tiers of thickly canopied niches.

RANWORTH, NORFOLK. C15 screen of traceried panels painted with pictures of saints. Parts of it form reredoses to altars.

RADWINTER, ESSEX. C16 Flemish reredoses with folding panels. Free-standing figures against shallow carved backgrounds.

painted panels consisting of five scenes in the life of Our Lord. At Ranworth, Norfolk, part of the chancel screen forms a reredos and is composed of traceried panels painted with pictures of the saints. At Radwinter, Essex is an impressive sixteenth century beautifully carved wooden reredos of Flemish origin depicting the story of the Madonna. It has six deep recesses crowded with wooden figures showing the Madonna as a baby and then with her own baby, marriage, death and funeral. By way of contrast there are richly coloured nineteenth century panels on either side, each panel painted with another scene from the Madonna's life. These panels were made to fold so as to enclose the precious reredos.

There are also some interesting nineteenth century reredoses, for example, Waltham Abbey, Essex, which contains four panels depicting the Annunciation, Angels and Shepherds, visit of the Magi and the Flight into Egypt. The stringcourse above has two Aesop fables, The Fox and the Goose and The Wolf and the Crane. South Weald, Essex, has a wonderful alabaster reredos on the lines of the Italian masters and portrays the entombment of our Lord.

Some further examples are: Smarden, Kent; St Peter Mancroft, Norwich, Norfolk; Worstead, Norfolk; Newark, Nottinghamshire; Chipping Norton, Oxfordshire; Axbridge, Somerset; Long Melford, Suffolk; Winterbourne Monkton, Wiltshire.

5

Screens and Rood Lofts

In the last years before the Dissolution of the Monasteries the interiors of English churches had become glorious to behold but what first arrested the attention on entering was the soaring Rood and Rood screen silhouetted against the beautiful colours of the stained glass in the great east window of the chancel. Almost every church had its Rood and Rood screen.

From the earliest times the apse or sacrarium in which stood the only altar in the church was protected by some kind of fence. It is known that old St

BRADFORD-ON-AVON, WILTSHIRE, (ST LAURENCE). Narrow Saxon chancel arch with through stones.

43

Peter's, Rome, had a Rood beam of silver presented by Pope Leo III (795–816) and it is, therefore, reasonable to suppose that as it was made of silver there must surely have also existed plain wooden Rood beams. The greater churches of the early Christians were all unvaulted and so the Rood beam was of wide span and unsupported and would certainly have sagged in the middle. To prevent this supports would be added in the form of columns which converted the Rood beam into a Rood screen. Such an erection was at once an altar railing and Rood screen.

Later, the chancels of these greater churches were lengthened to make room for the quires and just as the altar had been fenced off so the quire was enclosed often with colonnades supporting a parapet. Screens such as these were to be found in England in the form of the triple chancel arches of the earliest Anglo-Saxon churches of the seventh century. Remains have been found at Brixworth, Northamptonshire; Reculver, Kent; St Pancras; Canterbury, Kent and St Peter-on-the-Wall, Bradwell-on-Sea, Essex. Some of these arches rested on reused Roman shafts. After the seventh century the triple arch was replaced in Anglo-Saxon churches by a narrow single chancel arch. How early screens within a single chancel arch appeared in England it is not possible to say but it is known that there were screens at Canterbury in the twelfth century and at Bury St Edmunds in the thirteenth century. William of Malmesbury said in 1091 that, 'a flash of lightning broke up the Rood beam, splintered the image of Our Lord and hurled down that of the Blessed Virgin'. From this it is clear that in the eleventh century there was the beam and Rood which, in time, was to receive supports and be converted from a Rood and beam into a Rood screen.

The thirteenth century was a period of chancel rebuilding. Old apses and short single-bay chancels were swept away and were replaced by chancels of two or three bays in length. To the worshippers in the nave the most important architectural feature in the building was the opening leading into the chancel, the Holy of Holies.

In early days, the Saxon and Norman chancel arches were kept small and they had their air of mystery which, during the twelfth century was increased by their elaborate decoration. It is certain that this arch was usually closed by a curtain or veil in the simple churches of Saxon days. The survival of this curtain or veil in medieval times was the use of the Lenten veil whereby the high altar and its surroundings were completely shut off by a great curtain or sheet of stained or painted linen or other material which was hung between the sanctuary and the choir during the whole of the forty days of Lent. This Lenten veil was the reflection of what had once been the more primitive method of mysteriously shrouding the place of the Sacramental Presence from the main body of the church all the year round. The veil was suspended by

SALISBURY CATHEDRAL,
WILTSHIRE.
Lenten veil hoist.

AXBRIDGE, SOMERSET.
c. 1400. Squint to high altar.

45

rings from a rope or wire stretched across the chancel; the hooks or other fixings and perhaps the winch may still, occasionally, be seen as at Salisbury Cathedral. The regular use of a curtain or veil was thus relegated to a season of extra solemnity. King Alfred, soon after his triumph over the Danes in 878, ordained the very heavy fine of 120 shillings for the offence of tearing down the Lenten veil. By this date, therefore, a permanent veil must have become obsolete and as the veil for constant use disappeared a permanent screen with a convenient door in the centre took its place and prevented undue intrusion into the sanctuary. A considerable time elapsed before the Lenten veil finally disappeared, in fact well into the seventeenth century.

The chancel extensions of the thirteenth century had the result of removing the altar so far away from the congregation that they could not possibly see what was going on and to assist them openings were often made beside the chancel arch. These openings are called 'squints' but are sometimes referred to by the architectural name of 'hagioscopes' derived from two Greek words for 'holy' and 'watcher'. Squints are common and are of all periods being occasionally directed to a side altar but more often they occur almost anywhere. Sometimes a squint may be found directed to the site of the original high altar prior to the altar's removal eastward on the subsequent lengthening of the chancel. The majority were intended for the congregation to be able to see the high altar and thus view the elevation of the Host which was the most important part of the Mass.

Although the majority of squints were intended for the congregation squints are to be found in various places and their exact purpose is by no means certain. It is possible, however, to find a squint in the west wall of the nave which was probably used to enable a ringer within the belfry to have a view of the altar in order to sound a tower Sanctus or Sacring bell at the right moment during the Mass. Examples may be found at Brightstone, Isle-of-Wight and at Fen Drayton, Cambridgeshire. Squints may also be found in the north wall of a two-storey south porch which would have been used where the Sanctus bell was over the porch (Charlton, Wiltshire and Bridgwater, Somerset). There was no uniform position for the Sanctus bell which was sometimes in a bell-cote over the eastern gable of the nave, on the choir screen or choir wall, or one of the bells in the belfry or over a porch.

Sometimes the aperture is so small that not more than one person could see through it. In this case the squint could relate to a chantry. The most convenient site for a chantry altar was undoubtedly at the east end of an aisle of the nave especially where the chancel was without aisles. It often happened that the chantry priest would be reciting his office at an aisle altar before High Mass for the parishioners had commenced. The parish priest would object to

STEBBING, ESSEX.
c. 1350 stone Rood screen. Includes
ogee arches, some quatrefoil and
ball-flower decoration. Restored in
1884.

GREAT BARDFIELD, ESSEX.
Late C14 stone Rood screen. Rood
figures and central arch restored in 1892.

this and appeal to the bishop who would order that the chantry masses should
not begin until High Mass was in progress. The chantry priest in his defence,
would claim that when he was standing before his altar he was unable to see
when the parochial mass had begun and so to overcome this difficulty a small
squint was provided which gave him a view of the high altar.

In the thirteenth century the construction of the wide pointed chancel arch
destroyed much of the effect of mystery so it became customary to place a Rood
beam across from side to side and to fill the arch void above with a wooden
partition which served as a background for the Rood which was mounted in
the centre of the Rood beam. The term 'Rood' is of Saxon derivation and
probably from early times the image of Christ crucified or even the complete
Rood group of Christ, the Blessed Virgin Mary and St John was to be found
in our churches. The preference was for detached figures which with the rood
would rear in majestic isolation providing a visual focus for the congregation

47

who, for the most part, would not have understood the Latin services. This would be produced in two ways, the figures either stood on the rood beam above the screen level or else they rose immediately from the rood loft on top of the screen. In the case of a low Norman arch the rood beam would be placed above the arch, the wall probably being painted with the Doom, the final judgement.

During the thirteenth and fourteenth centuries there were screens of stone across the chancel arch with central openings and stone tracery similar to the style of a larger traceried window. The numbers of these screens must have been considerable but few have survived. In Essex there are two examples, Stebbing, *c.*1350 and Great Bardfield, *c.*1380. It is extraordinary how similar the stone screen at Stebbing is to the stone screen at Nidaros Cathedral, Trondheim, Norway. This screen stands out from the other architecture in the choir with its fine carving of foliage, flowers and ball-flowers which are typical of English Gothic towards the middle of the fourteenth century. The two piers on either side of the screen have round trunks with slender clustered marble shafts which have binding rings midway. The trunks have projecting foliage in the form of crockets which grasp around the binding rings, a similar form being found in St Hugh's choir in Lincoln Cathedral which leads one to believe that English masons were employed in the construction of the Trondheim screen.

The Great Bardfield and Stebbing screens show the same richness of design with luxurious cusping, crocketing and ogee arches but the Bardfield screen has the two main dividing shafts or muntins running straight up into the arch and the arch respond moulding stopping short with a stop which puts it into the Perpendicular period in the later fourteenth century, *c.*1375, and therefore later than Stebbing. The moulding of the Stebbing arch respond runs down to the floor without a stop and is therefore earlier, *c.*1350. The rood figures are a reconstruction of 1892.

The stone screen never became popular probably for two reasons. Firstly, the parochial screen was required to be so open that the view of the high altar would be as unobstructed as was possible and although this was obtained with the triple opening screens of Stebbing and Great Bardfield the stone screen did not, in most cases, offer an uninterrupted view. Secondly, stone screens were not designed to take a loft and this was the reason for their unpopularity at a period, i.e. fourteenth and fifteenth centuries, when the vast majority of churches had Rood lofts. It is interesting to note that Francis Bond in his book, *Screens and Galleries* (1908), says that before the restoration of the Stebbing screen it showed marks of having been cut to take supports for a wooden loft. In George Buckler's book, *Twenty-two of the churches of Essex* (1856), there is a plate of the screen as it was before restoration, showing the triple openings with slender clustered columns but with all the detail of the central opening which sprang from the capitals of the columns missing as, indeed, is the tracery of the two outer openings.

The entrance to the chancel of a church was always important. Confirmation and marriage are conducted there. In medieval times the nave of the church was used for many secular purposes and was probably the only public meeting place available in the village. For this reason it was usual to erect a screen dividing the nave from the chancel. There were also other reasons. The screen with its locked doors, except during services, served to keep the people, dogs and thieves from entering the chancel. It also defined the boundary between nave and chancel, the parishioners being responsible for the repair of the nave and the priest for the chancel.

The screens of the fourteenth and fifteenth centuries were constructed of oak enriched with beautiful carving and were coloured and gilded.

Devon has some fine, beautifully carved screens as at Marwood, which still has its original loft, Bovey Tracey, Chudleigh, Dodbrooke, Hartland, Ottery St Mary, Pilton, Stoke Gabriel and Whimple. Some fine screens may also be found in Somerset at Dunster, Minehead and Alford. Bedfordshire, Cambridge-shire, Essex, Kent, Lincolnshire, Northamptonshire, Oxfordshire and Suffolk also have good screens but this does not mean that interesting screens are not to be found in other counties although they are fewer and with some exceptions not so fine. For numerous fine screens, however, one must turn to Suffolk and Norfolk.

Suffolk – Barnardiston, Blythburgh, Clare, Cowlinge, Dennington, South Elmham, Eye, Hadleigh, Lavenham, Southwold, Sudbury (All Saints), Wing-field, Withersfield and Yaxley.

Norfolk – Acle, Attleborough, Barton Turf, Burnham Norton, Cawston, Corpusty, Earlham, Foxley, Happisburgh, Knapton, Ludham, Marsham, Nor-wich (St Gregory), Potter Heigham, Ranworth, Upper Sheringham, West Somerton, Trunch, Walcott and Worstead.

The fifteenth century saw the development of the Rood screen and loft many of which were provided by rich patrons. In this century the cult of the Rood developed with increasing intensity until the dawn of the Reformation. Magnificent screens with their lofts and great Roods were introduced into most of our churches. The Rood had now become an object of veneration and devotion contending even with the altar.

During the fifteenth century and up to the Reformation Gothic woodwork in our churches with its carving and colour decoration reached its apogee, brought about by the progressive skill in construction together with ever-in-creasing ingenuity. Although most screens are now in their original bare oak

BLAKENEY, NORFOLK.
Restored C15 screen
and loft. The Rood
beam above screen
level is original but
Rood group is modern.

state they were polychromed over gesso. Even where the wood has been scraped one can often tell that they were once coloured either by traces of colouring still to be found or by looking at the medullary rays of quartered oak and which, although normally lighter than the surrounding wood, darkens after paint has been applied to them.

The painting of the East Anglian screens is very fine and fortunately much remains, especially the figure painting on the panels which is elegant and graceful and together with the delicate flower and spray work which frequently forms the background to the figures these screens are delightful. A very good example of this is the beautiful screen at Ranworth, Norfolk which is probably the finest coloured screen in the country with its beautiful paintings of St George and St Michael as well as many other saints. The remarkable difference between

RANWORTH, NORFOLK.
C15 screen with beautiful painting of St Michael as well as other saints.

the Ranworth screen and others is in its composition in that it was designed
to include side altars and to form side chapels.

Many Norfolk churches contain screens with painted panels, for example,
Lessingham, Potter Heigham, Barton Turf, South Repps, Trimingham and
Cawston. Suffolk must not be left out with its screens having fine remaining
gesso work at Bramfield, Southwold, Gislingham and Yaxley. It is very possible
that it is to these beautiful screens that we owe the magnificently reconstructed
naves of our churches. If the screen, loft and Rood were to be exceedingly
beautiful and dignified it would not have been possible to construct them in the
comparatively low buildings of the twelfth and thirteenth centuries. A further
consideration is the Rood, the chief object and focal point. In the small dark
churches it would not have been clearly seen due to there being little light
high up. To overcome this, where there was sufficient money available,
clerestories were raised. Clerestories were, of course, used to provide more light
to the church when an aisle or aisles were added. Where, however, for financial
or other reasons the raising of a clerestory was not adopted other methods were
used, for example, inserting dormer windows as at St Nicholas, Ipswich, Suffolk,
special windows as at Wenhaston and Badingham, Suffolk, or small traceried

openings like the quatrefoil above the south transept roof at Earl Stonham, Suffolk. All these methods served to light the Rood so that it could be clearly seen by the whole congregation. The screen developed from the simple Rood beam on which stood the figures of Christ crucified flanked by the Virgin Mary and St John. The beam received supports to the floor and was frequently carried right across the width of the nave particularly in the West Country. The lower part consisted of a solid wainscot or panelling on which was painted figures of the saints or apostles or less often enriched with carved tracery all beautifully coloured and gilded. To enhance effect on some of the larger and later screens the backgrounds of the pictures were worked in gesso, that is, a plaster base made from whiting, size and linseed oil and applied in delicate relief, often being stamped with patterns while the gesso was in a plastic condition and then coloured and gilded. Sometimes the figures were painted on vellum or on paper and glued over older work, examples of which may be found at Cawston and Gateley, Norfolk.

Screens were usually divided into 'bays' with a pierced opening or sometimes a gate. A feature of East Anglian screens is that most of them are not fitted with gates and from their construction were never intended to be. Although this feature applies to East Anglia, screens in the south-west of England were designed for gates and most of them still remain. It would seem that the best efforts of the medieval wood carvers were brought to bear on the timber screens which in most instances show a remarkable display of their skill.

The earlier screens of the thirteenth century and early fourteenth century consist of a rectangular frame with a central doorway and two side bays with two or more lights or openings to each bay. The two sides of the frame are called 'stiles' and are morticed, tenoned and pegged into a horizontal head-beam. The bottom of the frame comprised a massive moulded sill which ran from end to end along the floor and on which was

EARL STONHAM, SUFFOLK.
Quatrefoiled tracery opening 15-inch square to give light to the rood.

STANTON HARCOURT, OXFORDSHIRE. Rare mid–C13 screen with squints.

RICKLING, ESSEX. C14 screen having broad divisions of four lights separated by shafts with shaft rings. Unusual tracery in form of squashed circles of reticulated window tracery having ogee moulding at top and bottom. Original hinges on doors.

mounted the wainscot which was, at first, plain and solid but later traceried and frequently decorated with painted figures. Above the wainscot the bays were divided by vertical shafts known as 'muntins' which were framed into the horizontal head-beam and the floor sill. The muntins were turned in the early period but later were moulded and instead of being framed directly into the head-beam, leaving plain rectangular openings, they were tenoned into a beam carved with a series of arches immediately below it. The arch-shaped openings were decorated with tracery, at first in the head but afterwards becoming more and more elaborate. Thirteenth century examples are rare and examples which are considered to be of this period are at Kirkstead, Lincolnshire and Thurcaston, Leicestershire. The Thurcaston screen is *c.*1300 and has a row of open arches. It is not in its original position having been moved to the tower arch. Stanton Harcourt has a very rare mid-thirteenth century screen with simple trefoiled openings and retaining its original hinges, lock and bolt.

In the fourteenth century and before the advent of the Black Death the building of screens began to grow and many of these simple but pleasant screens survive in East Anglia and elsewhere. Some very fine examples may be found at Fritton and Santon Downham, Suffolk, Watlington, Edingthorpe, Merton and South Acre, Norfolk and Guilden Morden, Cambridgeshire. Another screen of *c.*1360 is at Sparsholt, Berkshire, where it has shafts with shaft-rings instead of muntins and instead of pointed arches has cinquefoiled heads to each of the ten lights.

At the end of the fourteenth century when the country was recovering from the Black Death the great screen-building period set in and continued into the sixteenth century. Screen building, was, however, sporadic, as was church rebuilding, and most of this was commonest where there was peace and the land was free from the Wars of the Roses, where, because of the high price of wool the weavers and merchants were rich and people were of the opinion that nothing was too good for their religion or church. The vast majority of existing screens belong to the Perpendicular period but even in this period their progress was intermittent as was church rebuilding. Both were more prolific in those parts of England where there was peace and prosperity; where the farmers, merchants and weavers were rich from the proceeds of wool. Screens of this period are to be found in almost every county and though they are sometimes plain most of them are enriched with buttresses, pinnacles, niches and crocketed hoodmoulds often of ogee form with delicate tracery. The beams are elaborately carved with foliage. The screens of the eastern and central counties are usually more refined with delicate workmanship whereas those in the western counties are usually heavier and larger and in Devon often extend the full width of the nave and aisles. Most of the Devon screens fall into two types: (1) having the main pointed arch subdivided into two pointed sub-arches belonging each to two lights below with the spandrel between the sub-arches containing a spheric quadrangle which fills the space to the head of the main arch, as at Dunchideock, Devon, which is one of a number of fine examples; (2) where the central mullion of the four lights is much thicker than the others and is carried right up to the apex of the main arch separating the two sub-arches from each other. Many of these Devon screens are beautiful with their medieval colours and are, indeed, works of art.

As already mentioned the rood was originally mounted on a beam stretching across the chancel arch and these beams may still be seen in a few cases as at Tunstead, Norfolk, or the cut-off ends of the beam or the corbels of wood or stone on which the beam rested may still be embedded in the walls as at Nazeing, Essex. Throughout the fifteenth century it was usual for the figures to rise from the rood loft supported by the screen. It was the rood loft that

DITTISHAM, DEVON.
Early C15 screen across nave and aisles having painted panels. Four lights in nave and three in aisles. Fan tracery vaulting on west side.

SOUTH COVE, SUFFOLK.
Original rood stair door c 1470 with remains of painting of St Michael overcoming the dragon.

was so completely destroyed on at least three occasions that few English examples remain *in situ* or even in existence.

The first occasion was in 1547 when Edward VI ordered the destruction of all images so that every rood in the country with the images of Mary and John were removed. Queen Elizabeth, in 1559, added the following words to the 1547 Order, 'preserving nevertheless or repairing the walls and glass windows'. The second occasion was in 1561 in the second year of her reign when the ordering of everything above the bressumer, i.e. the load-bearing beam, be removed, that rood lofts were again attacked. On this occasion, however, considerable liberty was allowed to parishes regarding the loft and many parishes were granted permission to move their lofts to the west end of the church to form a gallery. The third occasion was in 1644 when the commonwealth ordered that all roods, fonts and organs should not only be taken away but should be defaced. This order was not always obeyed but many lofts were destroyed. It may be seen that the objection was not to the screen but to the Rood which it supported.

The majority of rood lofts have gone and sometimes the only evidence of the existence of a rood loft is the staircase which gave access to it. The staircase is usually a newell staircase, a stair around a central shaft and may be found in one of the aisle walls as in the ruined church at Covehithe, Suffolk, or Writtle, Essex or it may be in one of the piers of the chancel arch. Sometimes it may be contained in a staircase turret outside an aisle wall as at Hatfield Broad Oak, Essex. Occasionally two staircases may be found, one on each side of the chancel arch. These staircases usually had doors both at the entrance and at the top leading on to the loft but most have now disappeared. A few original doors are to be found and a fine example, painted with the figure of St Michael is still *in situ* at South Cove, Suffolk and another at Blewbury, Berkshire, which is nicely carved. Some staircases will be found having modern doors. Occasionally the staircase entrance was very elaborate and a good example may be seen at Totnes, Devonshire.

The construction of the rood screen and loft consisted of the top beam of the screen together with a further stout beam, called a bressumer, placed several feet in advance of it, which supported the loft flooring on which was built the gallery and on which stood the Rood. The gallery sides were protected either by panelling or open work but some were left unprotected. The top rail of the gallery on the east side was known as the candle beam as it was here that the candles were sometimes stuck in holes in the beam or access could be gained to a candelabra in the form of an iron hoop with prickets, to hold the candles which were used to light the Rood.

Another method of construction was that the screen supported a deep cove

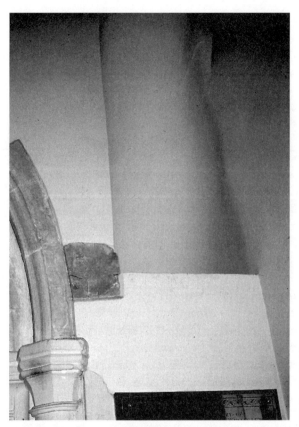

NAZEING, ESSEX.
Remains of loft beam and
rood stair doorway which
originally opened on to the
loft.

both back and front and this expanded top carried the gallery. Examples may be seen at Dittisham, Devon; Withycombe, Somerset; Bramfield, Suffolk (beautiful with pendant vaulting); Astbury, Cheshire and Charlton-on-Otmoor, Oxfordshire. It is this type of screen where the loft has been most frequently preserved, probably because its removal could not be effected without injury to the screen and, as already mentioned, it was the Rood to which exception was taken and not the screen itself. Most of those surviving are to be found in Devon.

If loft stairways are examined it will be found that many of them are remarkably worn. In some cases the treads have been resurfaced. The fact that they are so worn would seem to indicate that these lofts were in much more general and frequent use than they would be if the loft was mainly used as a place from which to read the Gospel at High Mass.

Evidence of an altar and/or piscina may be found indicating that occasional celebrations of Mass took place at the foot of the Rood. Examples may be found at Little Hereford, Hereford & Worcester; Great Hallingbury, Essex; Church Lawford, Warwickshire; Horningsea, Cambridgeshire and Oddington, Oxfordshire. There is also evidence in various inventories and parish accounts that some lofts contained organs, for example St Stephen, Walbrook, London and Hartland, North Devon. At Wimborne Minster, Dorset, eleven pence was paid in 1495 for 'glue and leather for the organ in the loft'. by the end of the fourteenth century choral singing was general in the abbeys, some of which had choir schools. In the latter part of the fifteenth century collegiate and parish choirs would be found in many churches. At Waltham Abbey, Essex, there were a number or organs, large and small, the small ones being capable of being carried and used in a gallery.

The candle beam, as its name implies, held candles to light the Rood and it was necessary for these to be serviced and for the Rood and attendant figures to be cleaned. Where there was an altar and piscina in the loft it must be assumed that on occasions the priest celebrated Mass there and as the staircase was narrow it must also be assumed that he vested himself on the loft and did not attempt to negotiate such a narrow staircase, usually having rough walls, in his vestments which were costly items and might be damaged in the process. As already mentioned choirs were becoming general by the end of the fourteenth century and they would use the loft, and where there was an organ, the organist would also use the loft. Small bands of musicians would also play from the loft on special days. It will be seen, therefore, that the loft was frequently used and this would account for the wear which may be seen on the treads, caused mostly, no doubt, by the hobnailed boots or clogs of the village choirboys.

It is interesting to note that in a number of churches up and down the country the lower panels of the screens have small openings pierced in them and which are sometimes called 'elevation squints'. Many of these small apertures, and in several instances there are up to twelve such holes in the panel of a single screen, have been cut through with care and occasionally assume the pattern of a small quatrefoil. In other instances the apertures are quite rough and may have been made by children. They vary in size from eight inches to two inches in length and from two and a half inches to one inch in width. Where the old levels of the floors have been preserved they are about the height of the face of an adult kneeling on the west side. Openings of this kind, for whatever purpose, could not possibly have been of general use and it is obvious that they were an afterthought and were made subsequent to the erection of the screen.

In East Anglia which was one of the most populated and thriving parts of England, glorious rood screens were more plentiful than in other parts of the country and the lower panels were, generally, enriched with costly paintings of the saints on diapered backgrounds and so the mutilation of such screens would not have been permitted. A great number of these painted screens are extant in Norfolk as well as in Devonshire. In the pre-Reformation church the chancel screen was the usual place for hearing confessions but there is insufficient evidence as to the real use of these apertures. If they were used for confession one would expect there to be only one penitent making confession, or maybe one on each side of the screen, i.e. north and south sides, and so there would be only one opening for each penitent who would be kneeling on the west side of the screen. The priest, on the east side, would have found it extremely awkward and indeed difficult to place his ear next to the opening especially when frequently there were return stalls on that side.

The possibility is that these openings may have been made to enable kneeling people to see the altar and more particularly the elevation of the Host during Mass, the lower openings being used by children. This would also account for such openings being found frequently in side screens before chapel altars as well as in the main screens. When the fashion for elaborating screens on a more substantial scale was the vogue in the fifteenth century, the worshippers who had been in the habit of kneeling during Mass at the east end of the nave or in the aisles, would find their view of the altar cut off by substantial panelling unless they were able to take up a position almost opposite the centre of the screen. In these circumstances it can be understood that the worshippers would be anxious to obtain an uninterrupted view as they had previously enjoyed and, therefore, might obtain permission to have openings made.

There is, however, another possible explanation. In the offertory rubric in the 1549 Book of Common Prayer those who wished were to place their offerings in 'the poor man's box'. This required that the communicants had to move into the chancel forming themselves into some sort of offertory procession, as the Royal Injunction of 1547 ordered 'the strong chest' in which the parishioners were to place their aims should be placed near the high altar. Those who intended to communicate were ordered to 'tarry still in the quire or in some convenient place nigh the quire, the men on the one side and the women on the other side, here they are to remain for the rest of the service'. If, however, the chancel was not large enough to accommodate all the communicants some would have to kneel outside the chancel screen. Could it be that in the small churches it was necessary for those communicants kneeling outside the chancel to have openings cut in the screen in order to see that part of the service which was being carried out at the altar? Perhaps one day we will find out the truth about these openings. (*See* the pierced quatrefoil squints in the screen in Stanton Harcourt church, Oxfordshire, page 53.

A selection of screens

Bedfordshire	C14 Gravenhurst
Buckinghamshire	C14 North Crawley – carved painted figures
Cambridgeshire	C14 Guilden Morden – rood loft, painted panels
	C14 Tilbrook – vaulted
Derbyshire	C15 Ashover
Devonshire	Early C16 Atherington – loft over portion
	C15 Dartmouth, St Saviour – coved top with floor of old loft
	Early C15 Dittisham – painted panels
	C15 Lapford – very ornate
	c.1350 Ottery St Mary – parclose
	C15 Trusham – restored
Dorset	Cerne Abbas – stone, restored
	C15 Hilton – part
Durham	C15 Staindrop
Essex	C15 Abbess Roding
	C14 Castle Hedingham
	C13 & C15 Finchingfield
	Late C14 Great Bardfield – stone, restored
	C14 Rickling – original doors and hinges
	c.1350 Stebbing – stone, restored
Hampshire	C15 Silchester – fine carving
Herefordshire & Worcester	C14 Brinsop
	C14 Pixley – black oak with entrance arch of naturally curved timbers
Hertfordshire	C15 Baldock – width of church
Humberside	C15 Flamborough – original parapet
Kent	C13 Westwell – stone
	C15 Shoreham – vaulted, fine carving, probably one of the best screens in the country
Lincolnshire	C15 Cotes-by-Stow – rood loft restored
	C15 Swineshead
	West Deeping – stone
Monmouth (Gwent)	Llangwm Uchaf – rood loft

Norfolk	C15 Barton Turf
	C14 Edingthorpe
	C15 Ranworth
	C15 Worstead – 1512
Northamptonshire	Part C14 Finedon – stone
	C14 Kings Sutton
Oxfordshire	C15 Charlton-on-Otmoor
	C13 Stanton Harcourt
Shropshire	C15 Ludlow
Somerset	C15 Brimpton – stone
	*c.*1500 Withycombe
Suffolk	C15 Kersey
	C15 Southwold
Sussex	C15 Boxgrove – parclose
	C13 Old Shoreham
Warwickshire	C15 Henley-in-Arden
	C14 Long Itchington
Wiltshire	C15 Avebury
	C15 Malmesbury – stone
Yorkshire, North	1558 Hubberholme

CANTERBURY CATHEDRAL, KENT.
St Augustine's stone chair *c.*1210.

6

Seating: Chairs, Thrones, Stalls, Misericords

In cathedrals a special seat or throne was provided for the bishop on the south side of the quire east of the stalls. Exeter Cathedral has a splendid early fourteenth-century seat which rises like a pyramid to a height of fifty-seven feet.

The most interesting episcopal chair or throne in England is the great stone chair in Canterbury Cathedral which is formed of three pieces of Purbeck marble and usually known as St Augustine's chair after the first Archbishop of Canterbury. In this chair from time immemorial, successive Archbishops of Canterbury have been enthroned. It is also called Ethelbert's chair as an old tradition has it that it was not only a chair occupied by St Augustine but that it was the throne on which the Kings of Kent were crowned and that it was given by Ethelbert, on his conversion, to St Augstine.

In Little Dunmow church, Essex, is a large wooden chair of the thirteenth century which appears to have been part of a stall. This chair is of great repute having been used for centuries to chair the successful couple who won the celebrated Dunmow Flitch Trial and carried home the flitch of bacon. There are two holes on each side of the front and back panels through which poles were inserted in order to carry the winning couple. The Court was held at the Priory at Little Dunmow and it is probable that this chair used to stand in the Priory of which the present church formed part.

In Sheering church, Essex, is a very early fifteenth-century chair which again was probably made from a stall. Originally it had a miserere seat but this was missing as far back as 1710 when it was reported that the stall was falling into pieces. It has since been repaired with a fixed seat. The arms of the stall were originally carved with four faces, a king (crowned) and a monk (cowled head on one side and a lady (uncrowned) on the other side, the fourth head having been broken off. The stall has now been given a fourth head to replace the missing one.

Tilty church, Essex, the 'chapel in front of the gate' to Tilty Abbey, now disappeared except for a few ruins, contains John Wesley's chair dated 1776.

The prior's chair in Much Hadham church, Hertfordshire, is late fourteenth or early fifteenth century. Originally it was one of a set of three stalls possibly

TILTY, ESSEX.
John Wesley's chair dated
1776.

forming a movable sedilia. The slots and disconnected mouldings where they joined the missing portions can easily be seen. It has a very tall back, sweeping arms and applied tracery forming a cusped arch to the top of the back and two cusped arches on the front seat panel. Aveley church, Essex, has a fine early seventeenth-century oak chair of a type not usually found in churches. The legs and arm supports are elegantly moulded and grooved and the frieze is foliated. It is possible that this chair came from the Manor of Belhus which was owned by the Barret Lennards. The house was demolished in 1957. Feering church, Essex, contains 'John Bunyan's' chair of the seventeenth century. This chair is an exact copy of the chair in which, it is said, John Bunyan wrote *The Pilgrim's Progress* and was made by a cabinet maker of Bedford.

At Hexham, Northumberland and Beverley Minster, Humberside, are two

SNETTISHAM, NORFOLK. C14 stone pillar seats.

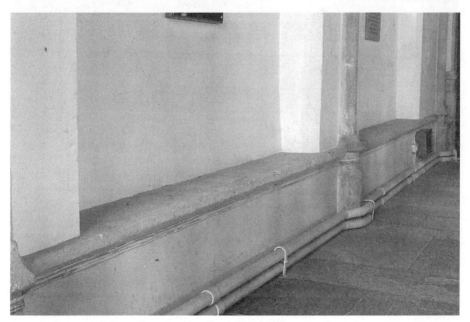

AXBRIDGE, SOMERSET. C15 stone wall seating.

remarkable stone chairs which are believed to be pre-Norman. The Hexham chair, believed to be *c*.681 was undoubtedly the bishop's stool in the early church being originally placed in the centre of the semicircle of the apse in St Wilfrid's Cathedral. The chair is cut from a single block of stone and is supposed to have been modelled from the stone chairs in the early churches at Rome and Ravenna. The edge of the seat has lines of moulding which also run up the front of the arms. The flat surface of the arms and round to the back of the chair are ornamented with a simple plait design with triangular knots at the back corners. The chair is known as the 'Fridstool' or 'Frithstool', a 'Stool of Peace' in which sanctuary could be gained if a fugitive seated himself in it.

The Beverley Minster chair is much plainer than the one at Hexham and was probably used by the official investigating the fugitive's plea for sanctuary. The privilege of sanctuary was granted to every church but there were special sanctuaries with special privileges of which Hexham and Beverley were two. At Hexham the area of sanctuary extended for a mile in each direction around the church and stone crosses were set up to mark the boundaries. The socket stone of one of these crosses which was removed from a field known as 'White Cross' is preserved in the ground of the General Hospital. The Beverley Minster

HEXHAM, NORTHUMBERLAND.
Saxon stone frith stool *c*.681.

Sanctuary Register for the period 1478–1539 is extant and shows that during this period some 460 self-confessed criminal fugitives sought the privilege of sanctuary. Rights of sanctuary were drastically curtailed at the Reformation and finally in 1623 an Act of James I abolished the sanctuary system.

Examples of additional chairs:

Desk and seat originally used by monks when studying in their cloister at Bishops Cannings, Wiltshire.

Chair said to have been used by John Wycliffe at Lutterworth, Leicestershire.

Elizabethan chair carved with twin greyhounds on the top and which have reference to the original owner at Puddletown, Dorset.

Two beautiful chairs having the initials I.H.S. and a scroll inscribed 'Ecce quomodo amabat' at Halsell, Lancashire.

Fine chair at the back of which is represented the Resurrection showing Roman soldiers and Christ revealing the wounds in His hands at Cartmel Priory, Lancashire.

Jacobean chair with carved eagles on the surmount and front stretcher and acanthus leaves on the arms. Nicely carved at Cobham, Surrey.

Stalls and Misericords

We would, no doubt, consider a church without seats as incomplete and so we probably take seating in churches for granted. Prior to the fourteenth century this was not so and it was customary, when not kneeling, to stand for public worship and prayer. There were few clerics of parish churches capable of giving a sermon and people attended church for prayer and so there was no real necessity for the provision of seating. As there was no general seating people tended to wander about talking and gossiping except when the Sanctus bell rang reminding them of their devotions.

Before the introduction of wooden seating a small amount of seating was provided in the form of stone benches around the walls and sometimes around the piers in the nave. These benches were used by the elderly and infirm who would have found lengthy periods of standing too wearying and it was from this practice that the old saying 'the weakest go to the wall' may have originated. Church porches were usually provided with a stone bench on the east and west sides of porches on the north and south sides of the church. West porches may have a stone bench on the north and south sides. These benches enabled people to rest themselves before the service began, especially those who had travelled a long distance,which was not infrequent. As stone seating is permanent there are a good number still to be seen (Sutton-in-the-Isle, Cambridgeshire; Snettisham, Norfolk; South Bennington, Nottinghamshire and Axbridge, Somerset.)

The clergy officiating at the Mass had their seats, which were known as sedilia, situated against the south wall of the chancel.

Wooden seating was first introduced into the larger churches in the thirteenth century, especially collegiate, monastic churches and cathedrals, in the form of stalls, strictly meaning 'standing places' and not 'seats', for the monks and canons who spent many hours of each day reciting and singing the offices of Matins, Lauds, Prime, Terce, Sext, Nones, Vespers and finally Compline. The stalls were arranged on either side of the quire in one or more rows, generally two, with returned stalls at the west end of which the two next to the gate of the screen were occupied by the abbot and prior or the dean and sub-dean respectively. The back row was a little above the row in front, the back of which formed the back row desk, the front row having a low desk in front. Each stall was separated from its neighbours by a curved back with elbows. These elbows are often beautifully carved with small figures. In the larger churches the stalls in the back row were covered by canopies. Some fine stalls of the fourteenth century may be seen in Balsham church, Cambridgeshire and Worcester Cathedral. Standing and kneeling were the only attitudes formally recognised during divine service. The rubric or directions demanded that the monks and clerics were required to stand during the singing and reciting of the daily offices which were carried out by night and day, commencing in the summer months between two and three in the morning and at intervals through the day until Compline at 8 p.m.

Indulgences were allowed to infirm monks out of mercy which to the stern monastic world could mean a glass of milk in the summer or an extra blanket in the winter or perhaps a portion of meat in the Lenten period, or, during the long offices, permission to lean on a staff or crutch and so relieve the weight on the legs. As already mentioned each stall had permanent arms on which the occupant could rest whilst standing. Sitting was not allowed until later and then only for the sick and feeble. With time this limitation was also relaxed for certain parts of the offices and so opened the way for the gradual development of the stalls. Even the rigorous Cistercians permitted occasional selective sitting.

The monastic life was dominated day and night by frequent and sustained periods of prayer and devotion during which the monks were required to stand. As the length of the services increased so the rule was gradually relaxed

BALSHAM, CAMBRIDGESHIRE.
C14 stalls having armrests
with two projections, one
above the other with human
figures or animals.

and any remaining embarrassment about the indulgence was finally overcome by an ingenious invention. This further and later indulgence or 'misericodia', 'act of mercy', was to construct the seats of the stalls with pivots and hinges so that they could be turned up like theatre seats. The underside of the seat was provided with a projecting ledge which gave a little support to a person standing in the stall when the seat was tipped up. These ledges were called 'misericords', 'indulgence seats', and allowed the person to appear to be standing whilst actually leaning against the ledge under the upturned seat. This support enabled the monks and canons to comply with the rule which required them to stand. Sometimes even with the aid of the misericord it was found impossible to stand during the long and numerous services and further dispensation had to be granted. At Westminster Abbey three monks who had recently had their blood 'let' did not proceed to the stalls for services but to a chapel where they were allowed to sit.

The stall seats were carved from a single piece of wood, usually oak, in such a way that a rough triangular wedge-shaped block or corbel remained underneath which carried the central ornament and supported the ledge on which the monk or priest sat. It was the corbel that was carved, firstly with simple patterns of foliage or sometimes in combination of foliage and dragons. Later these carvings grew much more elaborate and naturalistic until they contained a multitude of wildlife and domestic scenes. A unique feature of English misericords is the supporters that are on either side of the central motif and which sometimes relate to or are a part of the central theme. The fact that few sets of misericords appear to follow a consistent theme would appear to indicate that the carvers were allowed a free hand in choosing their subjects so enabling them to give vent to their imaginations. The subject matters were very varied but peculiarly scriptural subjects are rare. It is astonishing that carved works which were exclusively for the choir, the very heart of the church, should be of a non-religious and sometimes of an irreverent nature. Was it because these carvings were hidden from view that the carvers were given a free hand in the subject matter? All other carving on the stalls, particularly the upper part, contained religious subjects such as apostles, saints and prophets and was rigidly controlled.

The art of the misericord carvers was based essentially on life, the life they knew, saw and lived and so these carvings help us to understand the way of life and mentality of our ancestors. Much of this art was obtained from derived sources, from proverbs, folklore, fables and the Bestiary, a kind of naturalist's scrapbook which originated in book form between the second and fifth centuries BC and was gradually added to. The Bestiary contains information about fabulous animals and birds each of which is coupled with a moral and out of which arose a symbolism which is still strong in literature and legend and was used to illustrate a Christian text and the conflict between good and evil in the world. There are many Latin Bestiaries mainly of the twelfth century.

It is not easy to understand the imagery and thought processes of the medieval mind when we look at misericords. The interpretation of some of the imagery is extremely difficult and it has been said that so strange were the thought processes which lay behind it that a hundred years of intensive modern scholarship have still not fully decided on the correct interpretation to be placed on many of the scenes.

The subjects dealt with are numerous. They include:

1. Eastern mythology (St Michael and St George and the Phoenix)

2. Classical mythology, including mermaid, dolphin, satyr and wodehouses

3. Moral beasts, including lion, eagle, fox, serpent, hyena, dove, pelican, salamander, basilisk, dragon, wyvern

4. Medieval romances – Reynard the Fox, Valentine and Owen, Alexander's Flight, Sir Yvain, Lay of Aristotle and others

5. Aesop's Fables

6. Scenes from everyday life

7. Agriculture and trades

8. Sports and pastimes

9. Months and seasons

10. Old Testament subjects

11. New Testament subjects

12. Saints

13. Symbolism

14. Jousts and tournaments

15. Satire on religion

16. Moral lessons

17. Heraldry

18. Foliage and figure subjects

19. Nursery rhymes

In classical mythology the mermaid of all the subjects was the most popular, probably because her curving tail fitted so well into the available space. Normally the mermaid is shown with a comb in one hand and a mirror in the other as may be seen at Cartmel, Lancashire; Westminster Abbey; Ludlow, Shropshire and Ripon Cathedral, West Yorkshire. The mermaid is part of the mythology group – a siren who lures seamen, dragging them down to the bottom of the sea. The moral is that men are like mermaids, they speak fair but their deeds are evil. Sometimes the mermaid is shown with a fish in her hand, the fish being the symbol of Our Lord and so the fish being in the grasp of the mermaid symbolises a christian soul caught by the enchantment of evil. The supporters are frequently dolphins which are said to be attracted by the human voice. As the events depicted expanded so the supporters grew more complex, sometimes relating to or even playing a part of the central theme or merely complementing it.

Moral beasts were also popular and included the elephant, sometimes complete with howdah as at Beverley Minster and Ripon Cathedral, Yorkshire. The eagle as well as being the symbol of St John the Evangelist is referred to in many parts of the Bible and it is said in Psalm 103, 'so that thy youth is renewed like the eagle's'. It is said that when the eagle has grown old and its eyes dim, it flies upwards to the sun till it has purged the film from its eyes; then plunges three times into a spring of pure water when it recovers its youth. In this category one of the most popular devices was the satirizing of human behaviour through animal fables.

The Romance of Reynard the Fox in which Reynard instigates various cunning and deceitful acts used to warn of the greed and wiles of the wandering friars who had failed to adhere to their vows of poverty. At Castle Hedingham, Essex, a misericord shows the fox carrying off a friar upside down suspended from a pole over the fox's shoulder. The preaching fox was also a great favourite and may frequently be seen dressed in clerical vestments in the pulpit with a goose and a cock on either side (Ripon, Yorkshire). Sometimes Reynard pays the ultimate penalty of the law and is hung upon the gallows (St Mary's, Beverley, Humberside and Bristol Cathedral).

The pelican was another great favourite. St Augustine in his commentary on Psalm 102:6, 'I am like a pelican in the wilderness', tells us that the males are prone to kill their young by blows from their beaks and then bewail their death for three days. The female, however, inflicts a wound on herself letting the blood flow over the dead young and so bringing them to life again. The carving usually symbolises self-sacrificing love and the Fall and Redemption of Mankind. Usually the carvers only show the pelican reviving its young as at Castle Hedingham, Essex. Imaginary birds and beasts, mostly taken from the Bestiary, are also to be found such as the bi-corporate lion with large cupped ears and wyvern (two legged dragons) as supporters, as at Holy Trinity, Stratford-upon-Avon, Warwickshire.

The cockatrice or basilisk is another strange creature which symbolises the

CASTLE HEDINGHAM, ESSEX. C15 misericord. Pelican pecking its breast to draw blood to restore its young to life. (Fall and redemption of mankind by self-sacrificing love.)

Devil poisoning mankind. It has its origin in a harmless lizard which frightens its neighbours by puffing up the conical crest on its head. From this animal was developed the cockatrice which, it is said, and was indeed believed, was hatched from the egg of a cock at seven years of age. The egg was laid in the warmth of a dunghill and there it was incubated by a serpent or a toad. When the period was complete there was born a creature with the body and tail of a reptile but otherwise like a cock. So terrible is this creature that the most poisonous snake flees before it. As soon as it is born it hides itself but if a man sees it before it sees him, it will die, but if it sees him first, the man will fall down dead. It darts poison from its eyes and kills flying birds. Whoever wishes to kill a basilisk holds before his face a crystal vessel which not only protects him from the venom but causes it to be reflected and cast back onto the animal which is then killed. A reference to this animal may be found in the Book of Isaiah 11:8. Examples may be found at Great Malvern, Hereford & Worcester; Worcester and Exeter Cathedrals.

Among the medieval romances is the popular thirteenth century one about Sir Yvain who, on horseback, pursues a certain knight who on reaching the castle galloped across the drawbridge beneath the portcullis and takes refuge there. Sir Yvain gallops after him but as he rides in the portcullis crashes down

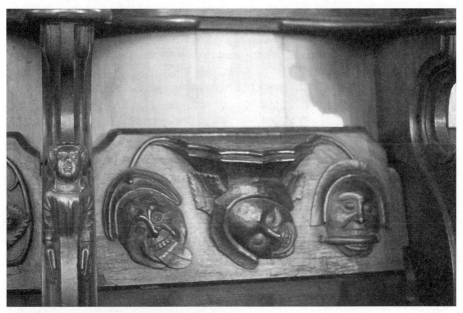

STRATFORD-ON-AVON, WARWICKSHIRE.
C15 misericord. Three masks of women grimacers (scolds – women who disturbed the peace). L. tongue out, mocking; centre, grimacing; R. successfully gagged.

and falls on the hind quarters of his horse impaling it. Sir Yvain is thrown into the castle yard and taken prisoner but a certain damsel showed him a way out and he was a free man again. The scene may be seen in Boston, Lincolnshire; Chester and Lincoln Cathedrals and New College, Oxford.

All the misericords I have, so far, mentioned have some symbolical or moral meaning yet there is a large and extremely interesting class which have no ulterior intent but are intended to portray faithfully the daily life of ordinary folk. The carver portrayed scenes of everyday life in the village, cottage or countryside. At Worcester Cathedral is a late fourteenth century scene showing a woman tending her cooking pot on the fire with two flitches of bacon and a dog or cat as supporters. Another fireside scene at Fairford, Gloucestershire, shows a woman with a distaff by the fire over which hangs a pot of meat. A dog has his paws on the rim of the pot and is trying to steal a piece of meat. Everyday country pursuits are common and two people may be seen at Ripple, Hereford & Worcester, reaping corn, each figure having a sickle in one hand and a wooden crook in the other. At Great Malvern is a man with a scythe representing haymaking in the month of June. The fox was very popular and is often shown running off with a goose (Gloucester Cathedral), sometimes being chased by the housewife with her distaff. Other homely scenes which may be seen at Fairford are a woman dragging her husband by the hair and beating him with a washing beetle, and a woman threatening her husband with a ladle while another shows two women sitting on three-legged stools preparing a bird for the table. These misericords show the fourteenth century primitive humour frequently to be found hidden in carving of this period.

At Ludlow, Shropshire, is a fine carving depicting everyday indoor life of a tapster drawing a flagon of ale from a barrel by means of what appears to be a spring-loaded device to control the flow. St George's Chapel, Windsor, Berkshire, has a misericord showing two gamblers sitting at a table quarrelling while the tavern cat takes refuge. Sports and pastimes of old England were also depicted and some interesting scenes may be seen at Bristol Cathedral. An unusual type of wrestling, where the contestants wrap a scarf or rope around their opponent's neck or a dual between a man and a bear. At Ely Cathedral, Cambridgeshire, the hinds are chased by the hounds and the huntsman has fallen from his horse. Another shows the harriers in an oak wood, one hare has been killed and is slung on a stick over the huntsman's back. Two hounds chasing another hare form the right supporter and another huntsman with a hound on a leash and blowing a horn form the left supporter.

Religious subjects are not so common as others but at Worcester Cathedral is the 'Expulsion from Paradise' showing Adam and Eve being driven out, Abraham offering up Isaac and the Presentation of Samuel. At Ely Cathedral

FAIRFORD, GLOUCESTERSHIRE.
C15 misericord – dog sniffing meat in pot while mistress spins.

we see Noah in his Ark awaiting the return of the dove which is shown in a supporter with the olive branch in its beak. The other supporter shows the raven gorging on drowned cattle. At Ripon Cathedral, North Yorkshire, Samson is shown bearing away the gates of Gaza and two other misericords have unusual scenes of Jonah and the Whale. The first shows Jonah being thrown overboard from a bird's-eye view looking down into the ship's crow's nest and the second shows him being vomited ashore by the whale. At Worcester Cathedral we have the story of the two mothers with one live and one dead child. King Solomon is in the centre under a tabernacle, flanked by his officials while he delivers his judgment. On the left is the woman whose child died in the night and on the right the official has handed over a large living child, kicking vigorously while the other woman has the dead baby in swaddling clothes.

In the fourteenth and fifteenth centuries painted figures of the prophets, evangelists, martyrs and doctors of the Church were popular especially in stained glass and stone carving but they are few on misericords. Of the evangelists, St Matthew is to be found at Cockington, Devon; Christchurch, Dorset and at St Gregory, Norwich, Norfolk – St Mark at Christchurch and St Gregory – and St Luke at Cockington where he is shown writing his Gospel. St John appears to be conspicuous by his absence although there may be one or two which are meant to represent the evangelist, for example, at Worcester Cathedral which shows a man writing a book on a stand while an eagle holds the inkstand. The doubtful part is what is the significance of the small bird being seized by a snake whose head protrudes from under the writer's hood?

Although the wood carvers showed little inclination to use their art to depict stories from the Bible or the lives of the saints they were very ready to portray moral lessons which they put in a plain and outspoken way so that the meaning could not be misunderstood. Every vice is shown in its natural ugliness. At Beverley Minster, Yorkshire, the drunkard is shown swilling ale from a flask while the devil is nearby ready to carry him off. At Blythburgh, Suffolk, the drunkard is shown in the stocks. Attacks on chastity are vividly shown as at Ely Cathedral where the lady defends herself vigorously, biting her assailant's thumb, pulling his hair and scratching his face. The domestic brawl may also be seen at Ely, the woman having seized the man by the beard belabours him with a utensil in her right hand. Then there is the scolding, shrieking, quarrelsome wife. If she was not prepared to take a thrashing then she must either be gagged and bridled as at Ludlow, Shropshire, or wheeled off to the nearest duckpond for a ducking. At Ely Cathedral two men are gambling with money or counters on a board. In the right supporter a man holds a goblet in his right hand and a pitcher in his left while in the left supporter is seen the wife with a hive of honey upset, symbolic of the fact that all her savings have gone in drink and gambling. Lechery is also featured by a naked woman mounted on a goat. Heraldic examples may be found, although not common, at All Souls', Landbeach, Cambridgeshire, where the arms of Thomas Arundel, Bishop of Ely and later Archbishop of Canterbury, are displayed and at New College, Oxford, which has the shield of Calverley, an ancient Yorkshire family forming the left supporter to the shield of Beauchamp of Warwick.

Finally, we find nursery rhymes and wise sayings. At Whalley, Lancashire, a misericord depicts the shoeing of a goose and shows the whole blacksmith's shop with the goose in the frame usually used for kicking horses. The blacksmith has an uplifted hammer and at the back are the fireplace, bellows, anvil and completed shoe. It represents a very ancient saying, 'He would flay the fox; he shod the geese, and tickled himself to make himself laugh.' The meaning is that if a man instead of attending to his own business, which he understands, tries his hand at other people's business, which he does not understand, he will make a failure of it.

In Norwich Cathedral are some sixty misericords containing a wide range of subjects which appear to have been picked at random. They are in good condition and can be ranked among the finest fifteenth century work of this class in the country.

The first record of the misericord was in 1121 when the Cluniac Benedictine, Abbot Peter the Venerable, referred to the existence of 'scabella', small sitting places attached to the seats as an indulgence and which replaced the leaning staff or crutch (example in New College, Oxford). The earliest seats with misericords have disappeared and the earliest stalls extant are of the thirteenth century. The corbels of the earlier seats were originally plain but the thirteenth century was a period which produced carving both in stone and to a lesser degree in wood. A few misericords of this period may be seen at Exeter Cathedral, Devon; Hemingborough, North Yorkshire and Sutton Courteney, Berkshire.

Dating misericords is difficult but occasionally the date may be found carved as at Ripon, North Yorkshire, where the dates 1480 and 1494, are shown or at Beverley Minster where there is a misericord dated 1520. Sometimes the name of the donor of the stall may be given and again this may be found as at Beverley Minster. Heraldry enables the name of the donor to be fixed. Costume is also a valuable help, especially examples like the woman's horned headdress at Ludlow which was in fashion *c.*1435. Where men are concerned the length of hair which was worn long from the first quarter of the fourteenth century until *c.*1400 when it became shorter, and the beard may be parted or forked and the moustache, is common. From about 1430 the hair, for the upper classes, was short but was cut to form a curious roll on top of the head. The hair was worn long again in the last quarter of the fifteenth century through to the middle of the sixteenth century. Armour is also a valuable criterion of date, e.g. the flat-topped helm seen at Exeter Cathedral is of an early date, mid-thirteenth century. At Chester Cathedral we see armour incorporating the jupon, a short sleeveless coat, and the camail, a mail apron fixed to the helm and covering the neck and top of the shoulders, *c.*1360. Later the camail was replaced by the plate gorget.

The misericord ledges of the thirteenth century up to *c.*1370 were rounded, plain at first but later having shallow moulding on the edge. The upper surface of the ledge became centrally hollowed making it more comfortable. After *c.*1370 they were mostly four-sided and often frontally straight but by the end of the fourteenth century they were variously curved or straight edged with moulding. By the middle of the fifteenth century there was another change with a thicker ledge covering the corbel which was carved in shallow relief around three facets (Beverley St Mary, Yorkshire). The ledges continued to thicken with more complex horizontal moulding.

By March 1540 the last of the great monasteries had fallen together with the greater part of the most wonderful woodwork the world had ever seen. Fortunately among the surviving churches were the great ones, both those served by canons regular and canons secular as well as those elevated to cathedral status, as were the former Benedictine houses of Chester and Gloucester. Many stalls in such churches were left unscathed but others were not. The popular St Thomas à Becket figures were outlawed by Henry VIII and were thus defaced or destroyed. There is, however, one remaining, reused as part of the lectern in Fornham, St Martin, Suffolk. Misericords were now beginning to be carved again and we find seventeenth century carving under heavy ledges at Wimborne Minster, Dorset, and at Brancepeth, Co. Durham. The eighteenth century also saw additional modern misericords at Arundel Castle, Sussex; Henry VII's Chapel, Westminster and St John's College Chapel, Cambridge.

When it is remembered how small an area the carvers were able to use it is astonishing that they were able to create such a range of subjects with such wonderful craftsmanship.

Examples of misericords of various periods

Thirteenth century

Exeter Cathedral, Devonshire.
Chichester Hospital, West Sussex.

Hemingborough, N. Yorkshire.

Fourteenth century

Leighton Buzzard, Bedfordshire.
Fordham, Cambridgeshire.

St Cross Hospital, Winchester, Hampshire.
Maidstone, Kent, All Saints.

Boston, Lincolnshire.
Hereford Cathedral, Hereford & Worcester.
Ludlow, Shropshire.
Worcester Cathedral, Hereford & Worcester.

Fifteenth century

Carlisle, Cumbria.
Bakewell, Derbyshire.
Ottery St Mary, Devonshire.

Auckland, Durham.

Norwich Cathedral, Norfolk.
Ripon Cathedral, North Yorkshire.

Castle Hedingham, Essex.
Ashford, Kent.
Tewkesbury Abbey, Gloucestershire.
Hereford Cathedral, Hereford & Worcester.
Hexham, Northumberland.
All Souls, Oxford, Oxfordshire.

Sixteenth century

Bampton, Oxfordshire.

Beverley Minster, Humberside.

King's College, Cambridge,
Cambridgeshire.

Aylsham, Norfolk.

Gayton, Northamptonshire.

Faversham, Kent.

Seventeenth century

Passenham, Northamptonshire.

Cartmel, Cumbria.

Lincoln College, Oxford,
Oxfordshire.

Durham Cathedral, Durham.

Eighteenth century.

Arundel Castle, Sussex.

Henry VII Chapel, Westminster
Abbey, London.

7

Bench-ends and Pews

A further type of church seating on which the medieval carvers practised their craft were the bench-ends of the benches provided for the congregation in the nave and which are now seen and admired by even the least knowledgeable of church visitors.

Sermons were the one form of public speech for which English was still used by educated men during the centuries when Latin and Norman French were the two dominant languages, but the coming of the friars, an Order living entirely upon alms in the thirteenth century, changed their character. The friars were able and highly educated men and they recognised the limitations of the common people to whom they preached. Not only did they speak in English but they used as similes things familiar to their audience. It is not suggested that all the scenes of sport, labour, domesticity and popular fables, which are to be seen depicted on misericords, were directly inspired by sermons but the majority of carvings could correspond to some simile in a sermon. One result of the increase of preaching, brought about by the popularity of the friar's preaching and the importance of the sermon in Protestant services, was the introduction of general seating into churches.

The earliest benches, about the end of the thirteenth century, were primitive, backless and with plain ends except, perhaps, for carved finials. Examples of this type of bench may be seen at Cawston, Norfolk. The majority of carved benches in England date from the latter half of the fifteenth century and the first half of the sixteenth century. Before seating became general some churches had stone benches at the base of the walls or around the piers, for the aged, infirm and women with babies who were unable to stand during the long services. Examples are to be seen at Tunstead and Snettisham, Norfolk; Tintagel, Cornwall; Sundon, Bedfordshire; Clifton Hampden, Oxfordshire; Patrington, East Yorkshire; Sutton-in-the-Isle, Cambridgeshire and Axbridge, Somerset. Unlike misericords, which are mostly found in cathedrals and the greater churches, bench-ends are not found in cathedrals because they have never had permanent wooden benches in the nave like parish churches. The finest bench-ends are just as likely to be found in the smallest village church, e.g. Bressingham, Norfolk and some unexpected discoveries may be made.

CAWSTON, NORFOLK. C15 backless benches with poppy-heads.

GREAT WALSINGHAM,
NORFOLK.
C15 benches with pierced
and traceried backs, figures
and grotesques on arm rests.
Fine poppy-heads, some
with a figure.

CLOVELLY, DEVON.
C15 bracket seats used by
pauper children.

Medieval bench-ends are not evenly distributed, some counties having more than others. The majority are to be found in Somerset, Devon, Cornwall and East Anglia and tend to be of a much higher standard than elsewhere. Large numbers were removed by the nineteenth century restorers with little knowledge of antiquity, in order to make room for the plain deal or pine benches uniformly produced in the Victorian factories. Why there should be this uneven distribution is not easy to explain. Perhaps the reason for the large numbers in the West Country is that both here and in East Anglia a great amount of money was spent on building and decorating churches at the close of the Middle Ages. As a result of the increasing prosperity brought about by the woollen clothing industry, large sums of money were donated by wealthy merchants and guilds, the result of which may be seen in the great 'wool' churches of East Anglia, the Cotswolds, Somerset and parts of Yorkshire of the fifteenth and sixteenth centuries. Some examples may be seen at Lindsey, Kersey and Lavenham, Suffolk; Walpole and Worstead (St Peter), Norfolk; Northleach, Chipping Campden and Lechlade, Gloucestershire; Wymington, Bedfordshire and Linwood, Lincolnshire. This prosperity led to greater demands for comfort and so it is easy to understand why it became fashionable to introduce permanent seating into church for the use of the congregation. The more prosperous the parish the more elaborate the seating and it is probably for these reasons that we find the best medieval seating in the West Country and East Anglia. It would seem that the provision of these benches often followed the rebuilding or enlarging of the naves of churches.

Several churches in the West Country have small auxiliary seats attached to the bench-ends which are often called 'servants seats' because they were used by the maidservants of the family occupying the particular seat. Sometimes they were just flaps which folded down or were boards which pulled out from a slot and had a leg support or were boards hinged to the bench-end with an iron leg support. Examples may be seen at Didling, Sussex and Gatcott and Tintinhall, Somerset. At Clovelly, Devon, there are some small semi-circular seats fixed to the bench-ends which were used by the pauper children who were brought to the church.

Styles of bench-ends vary from region to region, the two most apparent differences being that some, like the majority seen in the West Country, are square topped and only the bench-ends bear any carved decoration, whilst those in East Anglia often have the bench-ends and backs carved as well as having the top of the bench-end shaped into finials or 'poppy-heads', as they are called. The term 'poppy-head' has nothing to do with the flower but is derived from the French *poupée*, a doll, and refers to the figure carving often to be found in front or behind, or in front and behind the poppy-head. The majority of the English poppy-heads have simple fleur-de-lis finials. In other parts of the country both flat-topped and poppy-headed benches may be found usually without the same amount of detail carving. The flat-topped rectangular style of bench-end is attractive when used exclusively and when the bench-ends are in line. To reduce warping out of line, in the West, the ends were extra thick and they were framed with perhaps just a top rail or with styles. Originally the benches were raised on a low wooden platform bounded by a stout oak curb which would warp very little and into this curb the bench-ends were fitted. The bench-ends were, no doubt, raised to protect the woodwork from the damp floors. Where there were high curbs but no platform the curbs were used for the bench-ends and to contain the rushes or straw to keep the feet warm in winter.

The earliest bench-ends, that is during the second half of the thirteenth century, were usually plain and in the West rectangular, occasionally being carved with foliage or tracery. The East Anglian bench-ends usually had carved poppy-heads. The oldest bench-ends in the country are probably those at Dunsfold, Surrey of circa 1280/90, which have holes in the bench-ends to take candles. Incidentally this church still has three wood-lined 'plug holes' through the walls to act as drains when the church floor was washed out. The holes have chained wooden plugs but the holes have now been filled in to keep the rats out.

LAUNCELLS, CORNWALL.
C15 square-ended bench-end with symbols of the Passion.

WIGGENHALL ST GERMAINS, NORFOLK.
C15 bench armrest – priest blessing kneeling person.

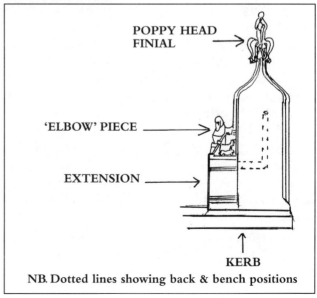

POPPY HEAD FINIAL

'ELBOW' PIECE

EXTENSION

KERB

NB. Dotted lines showing back & bench positions

Bench construction.

85

It was in the fifteenth century that the carvings began to show social interest and they are fascinating, only misericords offer anything comparable. The carvings illustrate a great variety of scenes of interest to church users and are frequently of everyday life, symbols of the Passion, religion, leisure pursuits, humour, fantasy and animals, birds and fishes. The carved bench-ends served as visual aids in a similar way to wall paintings, stained glass and the carving on the panels of Seven Sacrament fonts. As a Chinese proverb states, 'One picture is worth more than ten thousand words'.

The material used for benches was oak although there are exceptions of chestnut and beech. Timber was very plentiful in the south-west of the country and so it is not surprising that benches were made from extremely thick wood sometimes four inches or more and perhaps for this reason there is not much serious warping.

Many of the old benches have been altered, especially in the nineteenth century because they were so uncomfortable. The seats are usually about twelve inches wide and of various thicknesses, usually about two and a half inches but sometimes as much as four inches, but the benches in the Midlands are made of thinner timber. The method of alteration was either to replace or to fit a wider seat on top of the existing bench and to slightly rake the seat. In the east of the country the seats were very low and have frequently been raised but less often in the West and Midlands where they were of a more comfortable design. Other nineteenth-century so called 'improvements' included the removal of the floor platform either completely or else leaving the curb *in situ*. The side walls against which the benches abutted were often protected by panelling, the removal of which was another nineteenth century improvement.

Sometimes and particularly in Suffolk and Norfolk, we find that the benches have fretted back rests as at Wiggenhall, St Mary-the-Virgin and Wiggenhall, St Germaine, Norfolk. The bench-ends in these churches have lavish carving enriched with figures of saints in niches which are flanked on either side by armrests with seated figures. The tops of the bench-ends are finished with poppy-head finials in the form of fleurs-de-lis. Visiting the two Wiggenhall churches (St Germaine and St Mary-the-Virgin) is a 'must' for anyone interested in church carving. Other forms of back rest are comprised of either a simple long plank panel or vertical panelling with moulded top rail. The tops of bench-ends which are shaped into finials or poppy-heads are roughly of three types:

1. Trefoil composed of a central spike and a large crocket on either side which is usually turned downward (Tuttington, Norfolk).

2. Only a central spike without crockets (Aston Cantlow, Warwickshire).

BRENT KNOLL, SOMERSET.
Early C16 bench-ends illustrating
legend of Reynard the Fox in a
detailed and realistic manner. The
implication is not known but may refer
to a dispute between the parish priest
and the Abbot of Glastonbury.
(Top left) Reynard the Fox disguised as
a mitred Abbot.
(Top right) Reynard is foot-cuffed and
put into the stocks and a monkey
guards him.
(Bottom) Reynard is hung by the
jubilant geese.

3. Finial as a moulded base on which is carved an animal or figure (Blythburgh, Suffolk).

The first type is most common with its fleur-de-lis being very popular during the Middle Ages as it was one of the symbols of the Virgin Mary. Many of them were carved into foliage, often very crisply cut with fine workmanship (Fressingfield and Athelington, Suffolk – very fine).

It was firstly the crockets which were altered into heads and later into whole figures. A good example may be seen at Athelington, Suffolk. Another development was made to the shoulders of the shaped bench-ends. The difficulty was to provide for the framing of the back rail. If this was central the result would be a narrow seat and so in order to provide a wider seat and to conceal and support the projecting end, an extra piece of wood was added to that side of the bench-end. This piece, which is only found in the East of England, is

ICKLETON,
CAMBRIDGESHIRE.
C15 bench-end with fine poppy-head. St Michael weighing souls on one side and an angel with two Tudor roses on the other.

often referred to as the 'elbow-piece' but it can very seldom be used as an elbow rest as it is usually carved with figures or animals.

The carvings, both on the elbows and bench-ends, are well worth studying as they comprise, for example, a wolf with the head of St Edmund in its jaws (Hadleigh, Suffolk); Avarice, one of the Seven Deadly Sins, depicted by a man sitting on his money chest and Gluttony, holding a distended stomach (Blythburgh, Suffolk); St Michael, weighing souls on Judgment Day (Ickleton, Cambridgeshire); and everyday life showing a fuller in his shop at work with a mallet, an ale taster sampling ale (Spaxton and Milverton, Somerset). The ale taster had a very important public office in a medieval village.

Reynard the Fox stories appear on many bench-ends and at Padstow, Cornwall, Reynard is shown preaching to the geese in order to attract them close enough for him to catch one. At Brent Knoll, Somerset, are three adjoining bench-ends showing Reynard: preaching; stripped of his robes; in court with the charges being read out by King Noble, the lion; being placed in the stocks; and last of all the geese are hanging their old enemy. Animals and creatures of fantasy were also popular. At Upper Sheringham, Norfolk, is a cat with her kitten (elbow), a spoonbill eating a snake (Stogursey, Somerset), the Pious Pelican and her young which she has restored to life by feeding them with blood from a self-inflicted wound on her breast (Dennington, Suffolk).

Religious subjects are also to be found, especially Symbols of the Passion, such as the 'Five Wounds' (Abbotsham, Devon); Peter cutting off Malchus's ear (Frithelstock, Devon); thirty pieces of silver paid to Judas (Braunton, Devon); nails, crown of thorns, scourges and ladder (Trent, Dorset); pincers, ladder, sword and coffin (Launcells, Cornwall) and many others like the bench-end at East Budleigh, Devon, which refers to the woollen cloth trade and shows a pair of sheep shears and a sheep about to be shorn. The bench-end at Altarnum, Cornwall is carved with sheep. At Wendons Ambo, Essex, comes the warning against decoys which enable the devil to steal mens' souls. This is represented by a carved tiger forming an elbow on one of the bench-ends. It doesn't look much like a tiger, very few of the carvers had seen such an animal and could only carve from a rough drawing or description. The tiger is looking down into a mirror held under its paw. It represents the fable of the hunter who rides off with a tiger cub in the absence of its parents and baffles pursuit by leaving in the way large mirrors. The mother finding the mirrors and seeing her own image thinks she sees her cub and spends time in trying to get it out of the mirror.

The carvings are very varied and many hours may be spent in examining them in different parts of the country; also the different types of poppy-heads, elbows and the ends themselves. There are so many beautiful bench-ends to be seen and enjoyed that it is difficult to choose those of special merit but if I may be allowed to give a representative few of those with which I could spend many hours, taking in the carving, symbolism and craftsmanship, they would be Bressingham, Wiggenhall, St Mary-the-Virgin and St Germaine, Norfolk; Brent Knoll, Somerset; Fressingfield and Athelington, Suffolk; Abbotsham, Devon and Launcells, Cornwall.

It is interesting to note that when seating was first installed in churches the sexes were separated, the men sitting on one side of the nave and women on the other.

Pews

The term 'pew' originally meant a raised place or seat and so came to be applied to seats or enclosures in churches for persons of dignity or for officials. The triumph of the Protestant principle at the Reformation led to a rapid growth of private and lockable pews filling the aisles which had been cleared of medieval chapels and screens. At the back of the church stood or sat the poor and in between them and the chancel steps, carefully graded, sat the rest. Pews were situated in various parts of the church, at the west end, next to the pulpit, in the south aisle, in the body of the church, at the north door and in the chapels.

When pews were introduced the worshippers were no longer free to wander about the church, standing, kneeling or sitting on the floor, now, the pew or bench was disciplined and defined. There were bachelors' pews, judges' pews, pews for unmarried girls, for the parson's wife and, of course, the manorial pew for the squire. Some churches had free pews or at least benches under the control of the churchwardens who allocated them according to precedence. Pew spaces were sold and were an important source of income to the parish. They were let and bequeathed and became family possessions as well as announcing social rank and wealth. After obituary Masses were forbidden the lords of manors often retained the sites of their chantries and so a former chantry chapel might be turned into a family pew by the very family that had previously built the chapel, probably reusing some of the former stone and timber (Kedington, Suffolk; Wensley, North Yorkshire; Whalley, Lancashire and Stokesay, Shropshire).

In John Russell's *Boke of Nature* (1450) the chamberlain is instructed before his lord goes to church 'to procure all the things for his pewe and that it be prepared both with cossyn, carpet and curteyns, bedes and boke'. The apogee was reached when such pews became roofed with canopes and testers, fitted with fireplaces and cupboards and supplied with food and drink. After the Reformation and especially during the Georgian period, benches were gradually

KEDINGTON, SUFFOLK.
Bernardiston family pew constructed *c.*1610, part from C15 Rood screen which still
retains much colour.

replaced by enclosed seating known as 'square pews' or 'box pews' and were
satirized as 'horse boxes'. These box pews grew from the benches by raising
the height of the backs and fitting doors to reduce draughts caused by the
neglected state of many churches which were without heating. Box pews may
be seen in many parts of the country, e.g. Lower Wichendon, Buckinghamshire;
Llanengan, Gwynedd; Molland, Devon; Black Chapel, North End, Essex;
Stanmore, Greater London; Stanstead Abbotts, Hertfordshire; Worstead, Norfolk; Broughton, Staffordshire; Tunstall, Suffolk and Compton Wynyates
Chapel, Warwickshire.

In the country churches farms had their own pews, the family sitting with
their employees on benches sometimes arranged on three sides of the pew. An
example may be seen at Thurning, Norfolk. Some of the pews, especially in
farming districts were named with the names of farms or pewholders as at
West Grinstead, Sussex and Castleton, Derbyshire. Sometimes the backs and
doors were so high that they afforded complete privacy from all but the parson,
the clerk and the occupants of the squire's pew all of whom would be on a
higher level. The best bishops vigorously condemned these pews and Bishop

STANSTEAD ABBOTS, HERTFORDSHIRE. C18 box pews and three-decker pulpit.

SIDBURY, DEVON. Gallery *c.*1620. Enlarged 1754.

Richard Corbett of Norwich in a sermon preached in 1623 had this to say, 'Stately pews are now become tabernacles with rings and curtains to them. There wants nothing but beds to hear the word of God on; we have casements, locks and keys and cushions. I will not guess what is done within them, who sits, stands or lies asleep at prayers, communion etc. but this I dare say, they are either to hide some vice or to proclaim one; to hide discords or to proclaim pride.'

The fifteenth century churchwardens' accounts abound with references to pews which were allocated to those who could afford to purchase them and so we find entries such as, 'Mistress Abclyffe's pew – 1493', 'Mrs. Russell's maid's pew – 1467', 'Payd to a smith for makyng of a lock to Maister Stokken's pew … vllj'.

There are some fine examples of family pews to be seen, such as those at Wensley, North Yorkshire, C17 Bolton family, Kedington, Suffolk, C17 Barnardiston family, and at Rycote, Oxfordshire, there are two which replaced the Rood screen. The one on the south side is Elizabethan and the other on the north side, which is two storeyed, was occupied by Charles 1 who was twice a resident of Rycote Manor; Holcombe Rogus, Devonshire, early C17, Bluett family; Stokesay, Shropshire, late C17, Patron's pew; St Margaret Pattens, Eastcheap, London, Churchwardens' pews, C17; St Mary, Whitby, North Yorkshire, C18 Cholmley pew and a mass of galleries and box pews. This church was refurbished for Georgian sermons.

In the seventeenth and eighteenth centuries in a desire to increase the accommodation in churches without interfering with the all too ample proportions of the family pews, galleries were erected with a reckless disregard for the beauty and sometimes even the stability of the building. Arches were hidden, windows obscured or bricked up and piers called upon to have additional, and perhaps dangerous, weights. All this to ensure that the congregation in the nave might loll with irreverent ease. With the introduction of open benches in the Victorian period the need for the galleries disappeared and most of these have been taken down. There are examples to be seen at Biddlesden, Buckinghamshire; Stapleford, Leicestershire; London Colney, Hertfordshire; Belper, Derbyshire; Sidbury, Devon; Worth, Sussex and North Cerny, Gloucestershire.

During the worst days of the large private pews which were often partially screened from the body of the church, a special compartment called the 'Hall dog pew' was sometimes provided for the dogs of the local squire during service time. The dog pews were frequently found in country churches and were known to have existed at Aveley, Essex, until the end of the eighteenth century and at Northorpe, Lincolnshire, in the early years of the nineteenth century. In addition to the squire the members of the congregation brought their dogs to church, especially farmers who were accompanied by their sheep dogs. This practice was tolerated provided the animals behaved themselves. An important subordinate of the wardens was the dog-whipper whose duty it was to preserve order amongst the canine attendants at church and to chase them out when necessary. At Mullion, Cornwall, in the south door, is a dog flap to enable dogs to go in and out of the church when they felt the need, or was it to assist in the ejection of the unruly dogs? To assist him the dog-whipper was provided with an implement which consisted of crossed iron bars forming a lattice with handles at one end and forceps at the other and were known as 'dog-tongs'. Alternatively, the dog-whipper was supplied with a whip which was usually a thick stick to which was attached a stout lash or thong. These weapons were especially useful when shepherd dogs flew at each others' throats. Examples of dog-tongs, which are more prevalent in Wales, may be seen at Llaniestyn and Clynnog Fawr, Gwynedd; Llanynys and Penmynydd, Clwyd (Anglesey); Clodock, Hereford & Worcestershire and Bangor Cathedral, Gwynedd. Dog whips may be seen at Baslow, Derbyshire. At Youlgreave, Derbyshire, the dog-whipper's pew remained until 1868. It is interesting that at East Leake, Nottinghamshire, the dog-whipper was at work as late as 1842 and at Southwell, now a cathedral, it is believed that the position still exists as a sinecure.

MULLION, CORNWALL. 'Dog door' at bottom of south door.

8

Hatchments

The funeral hatchment, which originated in the Low Countries, is considered to be a shortened and corrupted form of medieval achievement but has come to be used exclusively for the achievements of deceased persons, i.e. the shield, crested helm, sword and other accoutrements carried at the funeral of a noble or knight, set forth on a large diamond-shaped panel. An excellent example of such accoutrements may be seen hanging over the tomb of the Black Prince in Canterbury Cathedral.

A hatchment usually consisted of canvas stretched on a large lozenge-shaped framework the sides of which were from four to five feet in length, although smaller ones are to be found. On the canvas the deceased's arms were heavily painted to withstand the weather. Occasionally wooden panels were used instead of canvas.

The hatchment was hung on the front of the deceased's house after his or her funeral for the period of mourning, some six to twelve months and was then moved to the inside of the church where he worshipped or of which he was

CANTERBURY CATHEDRAL, KENT.
C14 tomb of Edward the Black Prince, son of Edward III.

the patron or where he had his estates. Hatchments were first introduced in the early seventeenth century when the life of the Church of England was at a low ebb in the days immediately preceding the Commonwealth. No diamond hatchment has been recorded earlier than 1627. The practice is not obsolete and Peter Summers in his Hatchments in Britain series, states that some eighty examples have so far been recorded for the present century. Examples are at Deene, for John Brudenell-Bruce who died in 1917; Courtenhall, for Sir Hereward Wake, Bt. who died in 1963 and Great Oakley, for Sir Edward de Capell Brooke, Bt. who died in 1968, all in Northamptonshire. They are objects of great interest and importance to students of heraldry, genealogy and local history.

With hatchments the background is extremely significant so that it is possible to tell whether it is for a bachelor, spinster, husband or wife, widow or widower or a man surviving two wives. Rank may also be ascertained by the type of helm or coronet. The background to a hatchment is an important and unique feature as it is always painted black behind the arms of the deceased only, the remainder of the background being left white. The two halves are described as being on the 'Dexter' or 'Sinister' sides. The dexter side is the right-hand side when one is standing behind the hatchment and the sinister would be on the left-hand side. Therefore, if you are facing the hatchment the dexter would be on your left (the male side) and the sinister on the right (the female side).

The hatchment of a bachelor or spinster would thus have an all-black background. A husband or wife will have the background black only on the dexter or sinister sides respectively and the background of a widow or spinster is always borne on a diamond-shaped shield known in heraldry as a lozenge.

A shield divided vertically with each half bearing a separate coat-of-arms always indicates a marriage, the dexter half bearing the husband's arms the sinister half bearing the arms of the wife. This is known as an impalement: the husband impales his wife's arms. If a man has been married twice the usual practice is to display the arms of both wives. There is an exception to these rules in the case of a bishop. In this instance the shield shows the arms of the See on dexter with his own on sinister, the background of which would be black. The background to the arms of the See is white as the See does not die but lives on. The bishop's wife would have a dexter shield showing arms of the See and husband's arms as above and sinister shield with her surviving husband's arms impaling hers. The sinister background would be black.

If the wife is an heiress and can transmit the arms of her descendants it is normal, in England, for her arms to be displayed on an 'escutcheon of pretence' which is a small shield set in the centre of the husband's shield. Ladies are only entitled to put their arms on a shield after marriage and then only by impalement, otherwise they use a lozenge.

Sometimes there are small charges called Cadency Marks, usually placed in the centre of the upper part of the shield, as at Kelvedon, Essex where the cadency mark of Henry V is shown when he was Prince of Wales (eldest son). These marks were used to denote seniority of sons in a family but are now rarely used except by the royal family. Examples of cadency marks are shown on p. 98.

The peak period for hatchments was probably the late eighteenth century and early nineteenth century. The heraldry is rarely accurate and in most cases silver (argent) and gold (or) are replaced by white and yellow.

The motto below the shield was sometimes that of the family but frequently is just something sentimentally appropriate, such as, *Memento mori* (A reminder of death), *In Caelo Quies* (There is peace in heaven), *Mors janua vitae* (Death is the door to life), or *Resurgam* (I shall arise), which is the most popular. The hatchment of a deceased male

KELVEDON, ESSEX.
Coat of Arms of Henry V when Prince of Wales. Carved on eastern column of south arcade. (Cadency mark of eldest son.)

has a helm showing his rank on top of the shield. An esquire's and gentleman's helms have a closed visor facing the dexter. A knight's and baronet's helms have the visors raised and face the front while a peer's helm, usually shown on top of a coronet, faces towards the dexter and has a visor with five bars. The deceased's crest is mounted on top of the helm.

As a woman is not entitled to a helm the place is frequently taken by a bow of ribbon above the lozenge. The hatchment of a deceased married woman would show a shield with her husband's arms impaling hers. The sinister would be black with a ribbon bow over the shield with possibly a cherub under. A widow would have her husband's arms impaling hers on a lozenge having an all black background. A spinster's arms would also be on a lozenge with an all black background. Similarly a bachelor's arms would be on a shield with an all black background above which would be a helm depicting his rank.

Although there are many hatchments to be found in parish churches some have hatchments of old families showing the succession of members as one member succeeded another. Examples of this may be found at Theydon Mount, Essex (Smythe family); Brington, Northamptonshire (Spencer family); Compton Wynyates, Warwickshire (Compton family); and Trusley, Derbyshire (Coke family).

Cadency marks.

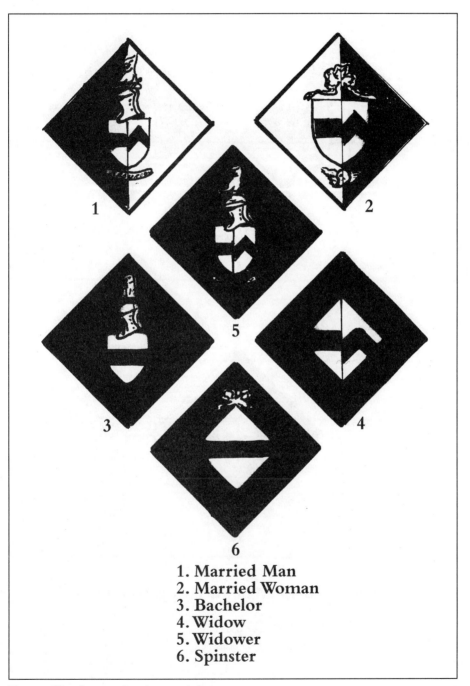

1. **Married Man**
2. **Married Woman**
3. **Bachelor**
4. **Widow**
5. **Widower**
6. **Spinster**

Types of hatchment showing marital status.

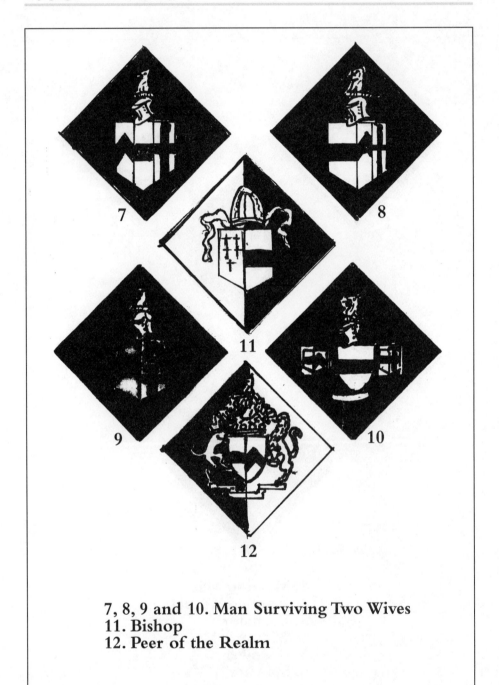

7, 8, 9 and 10. Man Surviving Two Wives
11. Bishop
12. Peer of the Realm

Types of hatchment showing marital status.

Helms and coronets.

THEYDON GARNON, ESSEX.
Knight widower died.

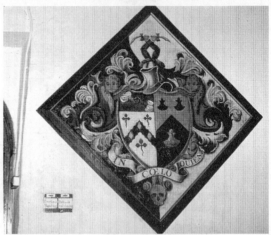

THEYDON GARNON, ESSEX.
Gentleman died before wife.

THEYDON GARNON, ESSEX.
Widow died.

MASHAM, NORTH YORKSHIRE. Wife died before husband.

THEYDON MOUNT, ESSEX. Gentleman widower died.

THEYDON
MOUNT, ESSEX.
Baronet who
had two wives,
died leaving
second wife.
Baron's helm.

TERLING, ESSEX.
Baronet died
leaving wife.
Baron's coronet.

9

Preaching, Pulpits, Hour-glasses and Lecterns

Although preaching in church did not become general until the fourteenth century it is a mistake to think that preaching was neglected in the Anglo-Saxon period or in the Middle Ages, circa 1066–1536 (for the purposes of this book), or that sermons were, in the main, a product of Reformation days. The oldest set of sermons preached in England, still extant, are those of the Venerable Bede (637–735), of which there are some 137.

The Anglo-Saxon clergy were encouraged to preach to their people and to teach the Creed and Lord's Prayer. In addition to the sermons preached by the clergy in the tenth century there was an abundance of homilies. These homilies were expositions of the Gospels collected from the writings of such people as the Venerable Bede, Herbert de Losings, Bishop of Norwich (1091–1119) and other theologians. Examples of these are the Blickling Homilies which were written essentially to prepare people for the expected end of the world in the year 1000 as well as the writing of Aelfric 'the Grammarian' monk and scholar (c.955–c.1020). Yet in spite of much preaching and the many homilies which were produced, heathenism died hard. The ecclesiastical laws of this period forbade people to indulge in the 'worship of fountains, necromancy, auguries and enchantments, sooth-sayings, false worship and legerdemain, or to bow down to idols and heathen gods or the sun or moon, or to resort to special stones and trees as holy places'. There was much ignorance and superstition at this time and there were many parishes where the clergy and people had been corrupted by war and neglect but the Church was aware of this and did its best to bring about reform.

Later in 1223 the Synod of Oxford directed the clergy to preach the word of God. Grosseteste, Bishop of Lincoln (1235–1254) directed the clergy of his diocese to preach regularly on Sundays and went so far as to draw up headings of the sermons for them. Towards the end of the century Bishop Quivel of Exeter drew up homilies for the use of his clergy. In 1281 Archbishop Peckham in his Injunctions directed the clergy to expound in the vulgar tongue, four times a year, the Fourteen Articles of Faith with regard to the Holy Trinity and Christ's Humanity, the Ten Commandments, the two Evangelical Precepts of Love of God and Man, the Seven Works of Mercy, the Seven Deadly Sins, the Seven Virtues and the Seven Sacraments. Despite all this effort new forces, both intellectual and social, were moving in the world, forces with which neither the parochial clergy nor the monks were fitted to deal. The returning crusaders, in the early years of the thirteenth century, had brought back strange heresies from the East and these found a fertile soil among the discontented peasantry of the times. The Church could do little, the secular clergy were far too ignorant and the monks too remote. A new type of Christian minister was required, one who would be under discipline like the monks and yet would be free to move about among the people whenever he could find an opportunity of witnessing by word and example the faith that was in him. This new type of minister was provided by the orders of mendicant friars, the greatest being the Dominicans and the Franciscans who provided trained preachers who travelled about the roads of Europe in their black-and-white habits, preaching, arguing, disputing, dealing with heresy and unbelief.

The first party of Dominican friars numbering thirteen, reached England in 1221, to be followed by a further party of Franciscans in 1224. They were welcomed by Archbishop Stephen Langton who was so impressed by their teaching ability that he took them under his care. From these small beginnings both orders spread rapidly. Henry III protected them, gave them money and materials for building and the people provided them with lodgings and money. Some of the more learned friars attached themselves to Oxford and Cambridge while their brethren were preaching the Gospel in the towns and villages of England. At this time a sermon was a rare event in most parish churches owing to most of the secular clergy having neither the ability nor the inclination to preach. The friars, however, were trained preachers who quickly attracted large audiences and made the drab services offered by parish churches more personal and vital. Everywhere, the friars made their influence felt and the country was ready for it.

Their popularity in the thirteenth century was, in part, attributable to their preference for going into the world instead of withdrawing from it, and partly because their poverty contrasted with the rapidly increasing wealth of the monastic foundations.

This high standard was, unfortunately, not maintained and whereas their only means of subsistence had been by begging they began to organise their begging on a large scale by appointing certain friars to see how much they could collect, even farming out the begging rights at a fixed rent. They began to keep servants, had better food and more comfortable houses which was followed by disputes and quarrels between various orders and between friars and seculars. From the beginning of the fourteenth century the influence of the friars began to dwindle and yet there is evidence to suggest that there was no significant decline in the number or quality of bequests and benefactors to the mendicant orders until the Reformation.

In the fourteenth century John Wycliff, technically a parish priest but in fact an Oxford don, spent most of his time disputing in schools and writing controversial pamphlets attacking the Church. These attacks provoked a response from the Church and in 1377 the Pope issued five bulls condemning the opinions of Wycliff who was formally imprisoned at Oxford. He appealed to Parliament and although a trial was staged it ended in fiasco. In 1381 he became rector of Lutterworth in Leicestershire and later died in 1384.

Despite his severe criticism of the Church and the papacy, a criticism which soon degenerated into abuse, as well as his denunciation of the friars, their apostasy and degeneration, Wycliff, with the assistance of some of his followers, translated the whole Bible into English during the last few years of his life. In addition he assembled a body of disciples who were prepared to go around the country in a fashion similar to that of the friars, preaching the Gospel. These disciples were known as 'Poor Preachers' and were mostly priests, scholars or just simple and humble men.

The revival of preaching brought about by the coming of the friars forced the parochial clergy to try their hand at a sermon, and so in the fourteenth century preaching became more common and books were written to assist them in preparing their sermons. This brought about the appearance of pulpits in a number of churches in England from about 1340.

As there were no seats in churches the people tended to wander about, talking and gossiping, but with the revival of preaching seating began to appear. The first pulpits were simple structures but generally they grew in size becoming elaborately ornamented especially from the sixteenth century.

The fifteenth century produced numerous manuals issued to help the clergy in carrying out the Injunction of 1281 as to definite instruction in the vulgar tongue in the main articles of the Christian faith. This was remarkable and clearly shows the reality of teaching and preaching in many parishes.

In the sixteenth century following the Reformation it is somewhat surprising that initially it led to a decline in preaching and in consequence to a similar decline in the making of pulpits. Freedom of speech was frowned upon and in 1548 preaching was forbidden except under licence from Edward VI, Protector Somerset or Archbishop Cranmer. The Injunctions of Elizabeth I of 1559 were for only four sermons a year to be delivered by a licensed preacher. Fear of the rival threatening influences of Rome and Geneva meant that licences were not fairly granted and the unlicensed clergy had to content themselves with reading a set of homilies. As a result few parishioners can have found sufficient inspiration from the pulpit to encourage them to spend money on new pulpits. Later in Elizabeth's reign, in spite of strong opposition to Puritanism, there was a movement towards a more subjective worship which we associate with Protestantism. The reading of the Bible and the preaching of the sermon took pride of place previously held by the sacrifice of the Mass. It must be remembered, however, that a beneficed parish priest did not require a licence when preaching to his own people.

An order of Edward VI that a pulpit was to be placed in every church proved insufficient but when, on the accession of James I in 1603, a similar canon was issued there was a flood of new pulpits and preaching enjoyed a remarkable popularity. Religious passions ran high and the English language reached its apogee with the Authorised Version of the Bible which appeared in 1611. The Civil War from 1642 to 1660 brought another period of restricted freedom of speech.

Sermons were as popular in the churches of the Restoration as they had been in the days of the Presbyterians. George Herbert, a parish priest and Cambridge scholar, had recommended the country parson to preach for about an hour and Isaac Barrow a seventeenth-century divine who enjoyed the patronage of Charles II and was known for his lengthy sermons, once preached a sermon before the Lord Mayor of London which lasted three and a half hours! Towards the end of the seventeenth century a new style came in, the old Puritan homiletic type of sermon which had become stiff and formal, full of commonplace expressions and pedantry, being rejected. In its place the new style was direct, clear, forcible and occasionally, witty. Although the matter may not have been very profound it was full of sound ethics and high moral code. Following the disastrous fire of London in 1666, the new churches were designed for preaching and therefore consisted almost entirely of a single large room forming the nave with a small chancel and sanctuary. There was a steady output of religious literature both from the Puritans and the Church of England. From the Puritan side came Richard Baxter, a divine and royal chaplain to Charles II, who wrote *The Saints' Everlasting Rest* and from John Bunyan the greatest allegory in the English language, *Pilgrim's Progress*. There were also vast volumes of sermons.

The early eighteenth century clergy were, as a class, unpopular, the rich being despised as ambitious hypocrites and the poor as ignorant peasants. Their reputation was that they were intolerant and quarrelsome. However, as the century progressed there was improvement and although many of the parish clergy were neglected by their bishops and were fighting a hard battle against poverty, many only getting £30–£40 a year, some as little as £20 and in some cases even £5, they did their best, as far as they were able, to carry out their duties faithfully. They visited the sick, relieved the poor, taught the children, conducted the Sunday services and preached the Gospel. The sermon continued to occupy an important part in the service and was still, by modern standards, very long. The sermons were limited by the hour-glass which the preacher had beside or on the pulpit but a preacher had frequently been known, when the sands of time were running out, to turn it over for 'another glass'! There was, however, little fire in the preaching as the Church was slumbering after the bouts of fever from which it had suffered for almost two centuries.

But this was not to last for long as John Wesley in 1738 had begun to make himself felt and in the Church, as well as the State, great changes were about to take place which altered the whole face of England. About 1738 he decided to take the world as his parish and he began to travel, mostly on horseback, up and down England – it is estimated that he travelled some 4,500 miles each year which he maintained for fifty-two years covering approximately 225,000 miles and preaching 40,000 sermons. He met with much opposition and no London pulpit was open to him. The clergy were often jealous and hostile and encouraged gangs of ruffians to overthrow his meetings.

As he journeyed groups of supporters began to gather together and Wesley soon realised that these groups would be much more effective if they were organised into societies. These societies quickly began to acquire premises for their meetings and much time was devoted to prayer and to the hearing of sermons. Wesley never allowed his meetings to clash with the divine services of the Church but eventually the movement grew so large and gathered so much impetus that the slender ties which it had with the Church were broken and the Wesleyans separated. Wesley's sermons were preached with great earnestness which was, no doubt, the secret of his success. His preaching, with intense conviction, attracted crowds sometimes numbering as many as 20,000 at a time when sermons in the parish churches were often dull and uninteresting.

After the First World War the distinction between those who worshipped in the morning and those who went to evensong disappeared and in its place there grew up a desire for one supreme act of corporate worship each Sunday in which all members of the Church could take part and this led to the popularity of the 'Parish Communion', the celebration of the Eucharist attended by young and old at about 8.30 on a Sunday morning. This led to the decline of matins which had some effect on preaching. Previously the morning sermon had been of considerable importance but now more emphasis was laid upon worship rather than upon homiletic and so in many churches there was only one weekly sermon instead of two. Effective preaching demands a regular congregation who listen to the preacher's message but the mobility of modern society threatens to undermine this. The modern sermon has also undergone change and is now much shorter although not always necessarily worse than its predecessors.

Pulpits

Early pulpits, even up to the fourteenth century, were light, movable constructions of wood which were mostly destroyed when more imposing and fixed pulpits came into fashion. It is said that Archbishop Arundel of Canterbury (1396–1414) preached from a movable wooden pulpit, an example of which is believed to exist in Hereford Cathedral.

Pulpits as we know them were used in monastic refectories for readings during meals long before they became customary in churches. An example may still be found at Beaulieu, Hampshire, where the refectory was left practically untouched so that it might serve as the village church which it has done to this day. This rare thirteenth century pulpit which looks rather like a swallow's nest, is still in use. Another example may be found at Chester Cathedral.

Most of the existing Gothic pulpits belong to the Perpendicular period and in this country are made of wood or stone. Although there are no metal pulpits to be found in England they are not infrequent on the Continent. Stone pulpits are comparatively rare and so far as I am aware there are about sixty remaining in the country. Gloucestershire and Devon possess twenty-one between them and the majority of them are beautifully coloured.

The earliest extant wooden pulpit, dated *c.*1330, is at Fulbourne, Cambridgeshire and there are some which are slightly later at Upper Wickendon, Buckinghamshire, and Evenlode and Stanton, Gloucestershire.

The stone pulpits are usually made of some fine-grained easily worked white stone such as Clunch (soft white English limestone) or Painswick or Beer stone

BEAULIEU ABBEY, HAMPSHIRE.
C13 monastic lector's pulpit approached by a graceful staircase within the wall.

CASTLE ACRE, NORFOLK. C15 hexagonal pulpit with painted panels of the four Latin doctors. Panels made up from screen.

CAWSTON, NORFOLK. C15 pulpit. Nicely traceried panels and vaulted stem on what appears to be the base of an old gable cross.

WENDENS AMBO, ESSEX. Fine nine-sided pulpit *c.*1500 with nine legs and elaborately traceried panels.

DITTISHAM, DEVON. C15 stone chalice-shaped pulpit, coloured and with statuettes beneath canopies.

and are chiefly to be found where this stone is easily procurable, as in Gloucestershire, Somerset and Devon. They are usually polygonal, having more than four sides, are attached to a pier or wall and decorated with tracery and colour. Examples of fourteenth century stone pulpits may be seen at Nantwich, Cheshire; St Peter, Wolverhampton, West Midlands and the fine open tracery wine-glass type at St John-the-Baptist, Cirencester, Gloucestershire.

All pre-Reformation wooden pulpits, except one at Mellor, Derbyshire, which is carved from a solid block of wood, are very similar and are distributed over the whole country being most numerous in Norfolk and Devon. Each consisted of an octagonal or hexagonal tub, tall and narrow with panelled sides supported by a slender shaft which, in the West, has miniature buttresses and panelling. Many of these pulpits have, however, been cut down and placed on stone bases. They are frequently decorated with colour and gilding and some in Norfolk have panels with painted figures generally representing the Evangelists or Saints similar to the screen panels.

The construction of pulpits is varied, the simplest form being carved from a solid block of wood, as at Mellor, Derbyshire. This pulpit is mid-fourteenth century and is hexagonal in shape and four feet eight inches in height. The panels are ornamented with tracery at the top and foliage work at the bottom.

Frequently pulpits were constructed with a separate slab each side or framed with sill, rail, angle posts and panels. These angle posts were sometimes extended to form legs. The pulpit at Wendens Ambo, Essex, has nine legs and the one at Mark, Somerset, has six.

In the West Country the stem or shaft support is stouter than those elsewhere and is mostly round. Sometimes the stem branches out into coving which gives the whole structure a 'wine glass' appearance, a name which is given to this type of pulpit. Examples may be seen at Stoke Gabriel, Devon, and Southwold, Suffolk, both of the fifteenth century.

A development, in the fifteenth century, was to have a canopied niche in each panel which contained a figure. These niches were very common in the West Country and the destruction of the figures at the Reformation was especially fierce.

The stone pulpit at Ditisham, Devon, is chalice-shaped late Perpendicular, with niches containing statuettes beneath canopies. At Trull, Somerset, is a fine, very early sixteenth century oak pulpit, beautifully carved and is probably one of the best pulpits in the country. It has five large statuettes representing St John with chalice and dove and the four Latin Doctors: Pope Gregory the Great, St Jerome in cardinal's robes, St Ambrose of Milan and St Augstine of Hippo. These figures stand on pedestals beneath crocketed ogee canopies and over the top of each canopy is an angel holding on to the crocketed canopy.

In addition, on each of the buttresses dividing the large figures are two tiny niches all containing minute figures of other saints. During the reign of Edward VI the larger statues were taken down and buried for safe keeping which, no doubt, accounts for their good state of preservation.

The medieval pulpit was intended to be a centre of attraction and the best of sculpture and carving was often used in its construction. Vivid colouring was frequently used on both wood and stone and there are many examples where traces of colour may be found. Perhaps the best example of stone colouring is at Cheddar, Somerset, where the pulpit is brightly coloured. Coloured wooden pulpits are to be found at Burnham Norton and Burlingham St Andrew, Norfolk; Southwold, Suffolk and Burford, Oxfordshire.

There are few known pulpits attributable to Edwards VI's reign but there are two which may be seen at Affpuddle, Dorset (1547) and Chedzoy, Somerset (1551). The Affpuddle pulpit was erected by Thomas Lyllyngton, a monk of Cerne Abbas, Dorset, who, at the Dissolution, obtained the vicarage; it has curiously carved figures in medieval costumes which are supposed to be intended to be St John the Baptist and the evangelists.

The number of Elizabethan pulpits is not large and the majority are dated. The reason that so few pulpits were provided in Elizabeth's reign of nearly half a century was that there was so little use for them. From the Conquest to the present day there was probably no reign when there was such a minimal amount of preaching, as in that of Elizabeth.

Just prior to Elizabeth's first parliament there was an indication of her attitude towards the Church. On Christmas Day 1558 she instructed the officiating bishop at the royal chapel, Oglethorpe of Carlisle, to omit the elevation of the Host in the Mass, which he refused to do and Elizabeth left the chapel. About this time Marian exiles were returning from Germany where they had gone because they were very afraid of the measures taken by Elizabeth's parliament. This was the signal for outbursts of theological argument which were not to the Queen's liking and attacks by pamphleteers against the hierarchy. To silence this uproar a proclamation was issued forbidding all preaching but allowing the Gospel, Epistle and the Ten Commandments, all of which were to be recited in English.

Elizabeth's first parliament met in January 1559 and passed two acts of supreme importance, the Act of Supremacy and the Act of Uniformity followed by a set of Royal Injunctions. Together these two acts form what is known as the 'Elizabethan Settlement'. The Act of Supremacy acknowledged Elizabeth as 'supreme governor' of both Church and State, but did not transfer to the Crown the spiritual authority in the Church, i.e. the right to minister the rites of religion which can only come from consecration, but it did transfer, as the

Royal Injunctions show, the right to make ordinances affecting spiritual matters. The Government tried to play down the injunctions in order to quieten public opinion on the Catholic side which strongly resented anything in the nature of a regal supremacy by a lay person over the Church. For this reason the title held by Henry VIII of 'the only supreme head in earth of the Church of England', which was carried on by Edward VI, was altered in the Elizabethan statute to 'the only supreme governor of this realm, as well as in all spiritual and ecclesiastical things or causes as temporal'. This difference in wording was intended to soften the impact on the Catholic conscience and to make as unobtrusive as possible the transference of ecclesiastical power to the Crown.

The Royal Injunctions which were drawn up by Sir William Cecil and modelled on the Injunctions of Edward VI of 1547 added new clauses which included regular preaching. Preachers were to be licensed and ought to preach in their parish churches four times a year otherwise a homily was to be read on Sundays. The universities and the bishops had power to license preachers but they used it sparingly in case the preaching should have a Puritanical or Roman tendency. Great disorder prevailed in the Church, some doing one thing and some another. So many changes had taken place during the last twenty years that it is not surprising that there was much confusion in the minds of both clergy and people and, therefore, probably a great deal of disobedience to the new laws. The commissioners, however, were concerned to see that uniformity was enforced.

The licensing of preachers did nothing to satisfy the need as a clergy list for the diocese of Lichfield in the last year of Elizabeth shows. The total benefices was 461 and the total clergy 433. Out of the total clergy less than a fifth, viz. 42, were licensed to preach.

The Elizabethan Settlement was, with comparatively little opposition, carried through, though there were problems ahead. The Queen kept demanding uniformity but to no purpose, for the utmost diversity prevailed and church life was at a low ebb in the early part of the reign. As time went on there was a steady improvement and clergy became more responsible and conscientious.

Further encouragement was given to preaching in a document drawn up by Archbishop Parker in 1566 known as the 'Advertisements'. These were intended to be issued as Royal Injunctions but the Queen refused to commit herself and Parker was obliged to issue them in his own name.

Many of the priests were ill-educated and ill-paid and their morals appear to have been at a low ebb. Improvement gradually took place and the standard of education was raised by the bishops who did their best to see that the clergy took steps to improve their learning and organised regular examinations.

TREDINGTON,
WARWICKSHIRE.
Fine Jacobean
pulpit with two
tiers of blank
arches, back
panel and tester.

Changes took place in the furnishings in the parish churches and pulpits were
built in increasing numbers. The Reformation had left its mark on the
appearance of the churches and in the form of worship. Despite strong Puritan
opposition there had been a steady movement from the sacramental worship
of the medieval Church towards the more subjective worship associated with
Protestantism. There was greater emphasis on direct communication between

the priest and his congregation and the pulpit acquired a more central role in worship.

With the accession of James I came a great change when a Canon of 1603 ordered that all churches should possess a pulpit and an initial trickle of new pulpits became a flood. It is these pulpits which are loosely called 'Jacobean'. The period was one when preaching enjoyed a remarkable popularity and men like John Donne (1572–1631), Dean of St Paul's, attracted large crowds by his sermons in much the same way as enjoyed by stars of sporting or entertainment worlds today.

A considerable number of Jacobean pulpits are scattered throughout nearly every county and the Laudian revival had a general effect on decency of worship which brought about the introduction of a variety of well-carved handsome pulpits. These pulpits were not so tall as the medieval ones, being low and bulky and easily recognised by the round-arched arcading on the panels. At Abbotsbury, Dorset there is a fine Jacobean hexagonal pulpit with double tiers of blank arcading. According to Dr Charles Cox in his book, *Pulpits, Lecterns and Organs in English Churches* (1915), the canopy or sounding-board had been removed. Is the present canopy an original replacement or a new one? Original canopies and testers are very few and I feel it must be assumed that the one at Abbotsbury is a later replacement.

The tester was usually large and supported on a standard or back piece, and was used to help carry the preacher's voice to the back of the church. Many of them are pleasing in design and decoration with shallow carving, chip carving, panelling or inlay work. Some have elegant stairways like those at Thaxted, Essex and Sefton, Merseyside.

Ashfield Magna, Suffolk, has a very fine and unusual Stuart pulpit. It is square and stands on short, hugely bulbous legs, complete with back piece and sounding-board and is inscribed 'W.F.' and dated 1619. Abbey Dore, Hereford & Worcester, has a good hexagonal pulpit *c.*1621. It has double arcading on each panel and stands on six framed legs. The tester has elaborate cresting and is supported by a standard with double arcaded panel similar to those of the pulpit. This type of pulpit was popular for almost two hundred years but gradually becoming less ornate.

The outbreak of the Civil War in 1642 to the restoration of Charles II in 1660 brought about a revolutionary period which restricted freedom of speech causing a sudden decline in the number of new pulpits, only about twenty-five being constructed. It must be recognised, however, that by that time there must have been few churches in need of a pulpit.

About this time the two-decker pulpit was introduced where the parson conducted the service from the lower desk and ascended to the upper for the

WITHERSDALE, SUFFOLK.
C17 Two-decker pulpit
having back panel and
sounding-board.

sermon. Good examples may be seen at Alstonefield, Staffordshire, which is dated 1637 and Brancepeth, County Durham, which has a pulpit of fine craftsmanship bestowed by Bishop Cosin who was rector between 1626 and 1644. This pulpit is made of richly carved oak having circular headed panelling and an elaborately carved cornice. It has a lower seat and desk and the fine standard, panelled with lozenge moulding, supports an ornate canopy or tester having pendants at the angles and carved with fruit and cherub-heads above which is a mass of towering pinnacle work.

In the late seventeenth and early eighteenth centuries three-decker pulpits became the fashion in keeping with the high box pews of the period. The high pews and galleries which were becoming numerous, necessitated the preacher being high up on the top desk. This type of pulpit comprised a pulpit

BRANSCOME, DEVON.
C18 excellent example of a
three-decker pulpit. Rather
unique in Devonshire.

occupied by the preacher, the lectern by the reader of the scriptures and the
Clerk's desk by the parish clerk who led the responses. The pulpit was often
the focal point of the church and a fine example of this may be seen at Whitby,
North Yorkshire. On the side of this pulpit is an enormous trumpet for the
use of anyone hard of hearing and not wishing to miss hearing the sermon!

These three-decker pulpits were furnished with fancy cushions, cloths and
hour-glasses. Bishop William Stubbs, a great historian, said that the pulpit
cushion 'seems to have been an object of special devotion'. In the 1725 terrier
at Northill church, Bedfordshire, there is an entry, 'A cushion for the Pulpit
of Crimson Velvet with 4 Tassels of Silk Twist; and a Vallance of the same
Velvet, with a fringe of Gold and Silk Twist'.

Some good examples of three-decker pulpits are to be seen at Salle, Norfolk;
Keddington, Suffolk; and Branscombe and Molland, Devonshire. The Molland
pulpit is accompanied by box pews of the eighteenth century.

By the early nineteenth century there was greater emphasis on the Eucharist so the altar had to become the focus in the church. This meant that the three-decker pulpit had no place and was reduced to a single decker on one side of the church, balanced by a lectern on the other side, at the east end of the nave.

Many of the three-decker pulpits were pulled down by the Victorian 'restorers' or were partly dismantled, the tester often being made into a table.

The very fine London seventeenth and eighteenth century pulpits must be mentioned. St Botolph, Aldgate, a Wren church rebuilt in 1741 with decorations of nineteenth century Classical, has a fine panelled pulpit. St Clements, Eastcheap, a Wren church (1683–7), has a really splendid seventeenth century hexagonal pulpit of Norwegian oak having oval panels and a huge tester carved with wreaths and standing cherubs. St Magnus-the-Martyr, Lower Thames Street, a Wren church (1671–1687), has a notable pulpit dating from Wren's time. It was originally a three-decker but is now a pulpit with a very large sounding board which is supported on a slender stem designed by Wren. St Mary-at-Hill, Lovat Lane, EC3, a Wren church (1670–1676), interior partly rebuilt in 1843, has a gorgeous interior including a sumptuous pulpit having a long wooden staircase with carved balusters and festooning. It looks more suitable for a private residence. The pulpit is panelled, the standard has bunches of fruit and flowers and the large sounding-board has bosses of flowers which project twelve inches. Finally, St Mary Abchurch, Abchurch Yard, EC4, Wren (1681–1686); the pulpit is 1685 and has its original staircase which leads to a delightful three-quarter circular area onto which the pulpit door opens. It is hexagonal with square panelling and a rather narrow standard which supports a large tester with pinnacles resembling an old tricorn hat.

Hour-glasses

The hour-glass, sandglass or sermon-glass came into general use in churches in the sixteenth and seventeenth centuries for the purpose of regulating the sermon. It was generally attached to the pulpit or to the adjacent wall within easy reach of the preacher. Large numbers of glasses and stands were destroyed during the senseless restorations of the early Victorian period.

There are records of hour-glasses being used at much earlier periods. In Allen's *History of Lambeth* it is stated that when a new pulpit was placed in the parish church in 1522 an hour-glass was attached to it. In the churchwardens' accounts for this church there are two later entries regarding the hour-glass. In 1579, 1s 4d was paid for 'the frame in which the hower standeth' and in 1615, 6s 8d was 'payd for an iron for the hour glass'. From the many references in the Elizabethan churchwardens' accounts it is evident that the hour-glass was the usual accessory to the pulpit.

With the restoration in 1660 the custom began to decline but at the close of the century new hour-glasses or frames for them were being purchased and their use became more frequent. This is borne out by the entries in parish records and by the general fall in their cost as compared with Elizabethan accounts. For example, All Hallows, Staining, Lancashire – 1561 – 'An houre glasse xijd' St Martin, Leicester – 1575 – 'Payd for an houre glass iiijd'; Ludlow, Shropshire – 1598 – 'For makinge of the frame for the houre glasse xxd'. Whereas in the seventeenth century an hour-glass at Seal, Kent, cost 8d in 1639; Bletchingley, Surrey, 7d in 1645; and at Chippenham, Wiltshire, 7d in 1657.

There is a story that a Puritan preacher having seen the last sands run out while his discourse was in full flood, quietly turned it with the remark that there was, 'Yet time to have another glass together', and so started another hour!

It is not to be supposed that because pulpits were supplied with hour-glasses that sermons were necessarily of this length although they were usually much longer than those of today. The glass of sixty minutes was probably regarded as a limit beyond which most preachers would not go. There is, however, record of a glass bought by the churchwardens of All Saints, Newcastle-upon-Tyne in 1632 which was made to run for 1½ hours!

The glasses were not always accurate and one East Anglian glass has been tested and always records forty-eight minutes. At Earl Stonham, Suffolk, there is a set of three glasses in a wooden stand containing one each for the hour, half-hour and the quarter. Sermons in the nineteenth century became shorter as Queen Victoria disliked long sermons and the pulpit glass

ABBESS RODING, ESSEX. C18 hour-glass and stand. (The hour-glass is believed to have been removed for safe keeping.)

EARL STONHAM, SUFFOLK. Late C17 pulpit. Iron hour-glass stand fixed to pulpit and a wooden stand fixed to wall holding a group of three glasses: quarter, half and one hour.

in the Chapel Royal of the Savoy in 1867 ran for only eighteen minutes.

It is the wrought-iron stands which are of particular interest and there are about 120 which still remain. Most of the glasses have either been broken, stolen or put away for safe keeping. The wrought-iron stands are examples of the blacksmith's art and there are some fine examples to be seen.

At Binfield, Berkshire, is a seventeenth-century elaborate iron stand with the arms of the Farrier's Company in London, with oak leaves, acorns, bunches of grapes, a lion, pelican and a wolf. St Nicholas, Hurst, Berkshire, also has an iron stand dated 1636 with oak leaves and acorns, painted and gilded. It is attached to an adjacent pillar together with a wrought-iron scroll inscribed, 'As this glass runneth, So man's life passeth'. South Ockendon, Essex has a small iron stand with four turned, wooden, baluster-shaped supports between the iron top and bottom. It is fixed in the centre to the adjoining wall so that the whole stand and glass may be easily turned over. Clovelly, Devon, has a simple wrought-iron frame which is mounted on a tall standard with spiral twist decoration supported on a base of solid cruciform brackets fixed to a cruciform plinth. Both Pilton and Tavistock, Devon have an hour-glass and stand held by a metal arm, attached to each of their pulpits. Perhaps the most ingenious stand is at Compton Bassett, Wiltshire. It has elaborate finials at top and bottom and incorporates a large three-dimensional fleur-de-lis rising from the centre of the stand and which serves as a handle enabling the preacher to reverse the glass and stand for a 'second glass'.

IO

Lecterns and Chained Books

L ectern was the old English word for a book desk which, in pre-Reformation
days stood in the chancel to hold the service book or for the chanters of
choirs singing the Gospel at Divine Service or Mass. One of these may be
seen at Ranworth, Norfolk. Painted on it is a biblical verse set to the old
musical notation of plainsong. The desk, which is fifteenth century, used to

RANWORTH, NORFOLK.
C15 Cantor's desk showing
traces of former colouring.
Two desks at different levels
on one of which is painted
a versicle with the old
musical notation. Desk used
to stand on the rood loft.

126

HADSTOCK, ESSEX.
C15 wooden lectern on
octagonal concave-sided base.

stand on the roof loft and has desks at two levels for standing or kneeling. Many of the medieval wooden lecterns have two desks but not at different levels like Ranworth. Ridgewell and Hadstock, Essex are examples.

The oldest lecterns left in Britain are made of stone circa 1200 and may be seen at Norton and Crowle, Hereford and Worcester. The late twelfth century Norton lectern is carved in white limestone with branches and leaves in stiff-leaf tradition and on the west side is carved a figure of a bishop (? abbot) in high relief, in his robes giving the blessing with his right hand and holding his crozier in his left. The sloping desk has a projecting rim to hold a book and the sides are carved with foliage scrolls also in high relief with animal heads projecting from the foliage on the north and south sides whilst on the east there are two human heads. The shaft and capital are modern. This lectern was dug up in the churchyard of Evesham Abbey in 1813 and some fifty years later was set on a new pillar and base and given to Norton church.

The lectern in the parish church of Crowle is partly thirteenth century and carved out of a block of blue-grey limestone with a sunk, sloping face to receive a book. The carving is in very high relief and on the west side there is the conventional vine which covers the lectern. In the centre is a beardless, draped figure with bent knees, who appears to be holding, precariously, on to the vine branches with both hands. The desk is supported by a central and four angle shafts having foliated capitals. The shafts are modern and were fitted in 1845 when the lectern, which had lain in the churchyard for many years, was restored. It is believed to have been brought to Crowle from Pershore Abbey.

Another example may be found in the prior's chapel at Much Wenlock, Shropshire, where the desk is carved with twisted conventional foliage and is probably of early thirteenth century date.

Sometimes stone Gospel lecterns are of a simple character, taking the form

EAST BRENT, SOMERSET.
C15 wooden eagle lectern
having a large heavy baluster
stem.

of a small desk projecting from the north wall of the chancel as at Etwall, Derbyshire and Doddington, Kent.

The fourteenth century heralded in the making of the first surviving lecterns of two types which have remained with us ever since: the desk-top and the eagle. Both of these appear in wood and brass before and after the Reformation but only some twenty wooden and about forty brass medieval eagle lecterns are left in the whole country.

There are two good examples of wooden lecterns, one at Leighton Buzzard, Bedfordshire, which is carved as an eagle with outstretched wings and which may go back as far as the thirteenth century. Attached to it is still part of the chain that held the old bible. The other is at Ottery St Mary, Devon. It is one of the earliest in England and is a gilded wooden eagle lectern standing on a globe on the side of which are the arms of Bishop Grandison who became

Bishop of Exeter in 1328. It is believed that it may have originally been above the stone rood screen which was across the entrance to the chancel until the early nineteenth century. Ottery St Mary was a collegiate church prior to the Reformation and it was usual, on certain days, to read the Epistle and Gospel from the Rood loft.

Occasionally the pelican in her piety, that is, shown pecking her breast to draw blood to feed her young, was used instead of the eagle. For example, in Norwich Cathedral, Norfolk, Middleton, Hampshire and in East Leake, Nottinghamshire, are the remains of an old wooden pelican which formerly formed part of a lectern.

Eagles were the most popular sym-bolising the Apostle John and the car-rying of the Gospel to the four corners of the earth and were considered, in

OTTERY ST MARY, DEVON. C14 gilded wooden eagle lectern. Originally featherless. One of earliest in England.

the medieval bestiaries, to be the birds which soared highest in the sky and were, therefore, nearest to Heaven.

The use of the emblem of the eagle in wood for lecterns was probably far commoner in England in medieval days than those of brass. Wood, however, being more perishable than brass it could more easily be destroyed. It is interesting to note, when looking at wooden eagles, how much easier it is to reproduce the plumage in wood than in metal as well as being a far less expensive material. The craftsman working with wood could far more easily produce desired effects than could be obtained in metal. Some surviving old wooden eagles may be seen at: Astbury, Cheshire (C17); Bigbury, Devon (C16); East Brent, Somerset (early C15); Leverington, Cambridgeshire (late C15); Sparsholt, Oxfordshire (C14); Wheathampstead, Hertfordshire (C15); Winchester, St Cross, Hampshire (late C14); Dettling, Kent (mid-C14).

Brass lecterns were also of the desk-top or eagle type, the eagle, however being the favourite choice through the Middle Ages for the reasons I have already given. In addition to brass lecterns some were made of latten like the monumental brasses. It is strange that the eagle and its symbolism did not incite the vandal Puritans in the sixteenth century as did the sight of the Cross and Crucifix. The fact that monks were prone to throw their valuable brass eagles into the nearest pond, was not through fear of their mutilation or destruction, but to cheat the avaricious king's looting commissioners of their spoil.

Most of the early eagle lecterns, whether wood or metal, have disappeared but there are a few of the fourteenth century still remaining as, for example, Norwich Cathedral, *c.*1375 which is surmounted by a pelican in her piety. Round the supporting shaft, at the base, are three small figures of a bishop, priest and deacon which were added in 1845 and look rather out of place. At Southwell Cathedral, Nottinghamshire, is a fine brass eagle *c.*1500 which came from Newstead Abbey, Nottinghamshire. At the Dissolution the lectern, together with some candlesticks were thrown into the fishpond. In the eighteenth century the lectern was recovered and passed into the hands of a Nottingham dealer. Later in 1805 it was presented to Southwell Minster by Sir Richard Kay, Prebendary of Durham. The beak of the eagle is open sufficiently to allow a coin to be dropped in and under the tail is a kind of small trapdoor so that the money may be withdrawn. It was probably used for the reception of special offerings. A further eagle lectern, which was also thrown into the adjacent fen to hide it from the king's agents, is in Isleham church, Cambridgeshire. It was found in the mid-nineteenth century. This eagle was also originally made as a receptacle for donations.

Oxborough church, Norfolk, also has an eagle lectern *c.*1500 having a slot in the beak for coins and an opening at the tail for removing them. It is a fine specimen, the lectern being six feet in height from the base to the eagle's head. The base is also supported by three lions which may be found on lecterns of this period. Bovey Tracey, Devon, has a fine brass eagle of the fifteenth century which has silver claws and three lions at the base. The stem has bands of projecting mouldings which follow the usual pattern. This lectern is very

(Top left) CAVENDISH, SUFFOLK. C16 brass eagle lectern. Said to have been presented by Elizabeth I.

(Top right) OXBOROUGH, NORFOLK. C15 brass eagle lectern. Also meant as an alms box. Six feet high with base supported by three lions.

(Left) SNETTISHAM, NORFOLK. C16 brass eagle lectern with three lions at base.

STANSTED MOUNTFITCHET,
ESSEX (ST JOHN THE
EVANGELIST).
C19 brass double desk-top
lectern.

similar to the one at Chipping Campden, Gloucestershire, which is about a century later.

The eighteenth century lecterns were mostly of the traditional type but there were variations. At Blankney, Lincolnshire, the eagle has a claw on a serpent symbolising the triumph of God's word over the Devil. Perhaps the most unusual lectern of this period is at West Wycombe, Buckinghamshire. The desk is formed by a small brass eagle standing on a sphere on top of a fluted stem mounted on a semicircular projection to a square platform which is movable and has carrying handles. On the platform is a Chippendale-style armchair in rosewood, finely carved and with cushion. The cresting is surmounted by a further eagle with outstretched wings. It is not surprising to find such a curious lectern in this church when one remembers the man who was responsible. Sir Francis Dashwood who was Chancellor of the Exchequer in 1762, was a man of great vanity and it was he who refashioned the nave of the old fourteenth century church into an eighteenth century fantasy containing painted ceiling, oak columns, cherubs carved by Grinling Gibbons on each side of the east window, three Chippendale-type armchairs and a font bowl of silver gilt. He also had the tower raised in height and surmounted by an immense gilded ball capable of holding ten men inside!

The nineteenth and twentieth centuries also provided some originality as at East Hendred, Berkshire, where the stem rises from a foot with a shoe stepping on three crocodiles. At Bridgnorth, Shropshire, the lectern is a whole figure of an angel with large wings. St Osmund, Parkstone, Dorset, has a reading desk lectern, 1926, forming a cage of hand-beaten bronze with twin candlesticks. To end, one must not overlook the unusual iron eagle at Attleborough, Norfolk, made in 1816. There are two fine wooden lecterns of the Victorian period, one at Sidbury, Devon, which has a double desk-top and the other at Navestock, Essex, which has an eagle.

Chained Books

It has been the opinion of many people that the chaining of books in a church originated with Henry VIII's Order of 1537 as to the placing of Bibles in churches for the use of the parishioners and because printed books were so valuable. This, however, is not the case as chained books were already in our churches prior to the Reformation.

Monasteries were the chief homes of English books in medieval days and their destruction was a great blow to literary culture. It was, indeed fortunate, however, that the custom of storing manuscripts, other than service books, in our cathedrals as well as in the more important parish churches, was well established long before the break-up of the domestic libraries. The library at Salisbury Cathedral contains some very rare books and documents such as one of the original copies of the *Magna Carta*. One of the men, William Longwood, whose name is mentioned in it, who saw it sealed, and had a copy made on a single sheet of about one thousand words, lies under the same roof. This copy is one of four known copies, one other being in Lincoln Cathedral and two in London. One of the books in the library is the one bound for Henry VIII by his own binder and was the King's copy of the book against Luther for which the Pope gave Henry the title of Defender of the Faith. Another is a ninth century copy of the Psalms. The greatest treasures of the library are the manuscript books, the earliest of which is the *Anglo Saxon Gospels* of the eighth or ninth centuries written in Latin with three of the original four decorated pages. On the fly-leaf are two records in Anglo-Saxon proving that the volume was in the possession of the Saxon cathedral.

CIRENCESTER, GLOUCESTERSHIRE (ST JOHN THE BAPTIST).
C15 chained books.

One of the canons of Salisbury Cathedral on his death in 1452 left some books to the library. In two of the volumes there were some notes written in the fifteenth century on the inside of the covers requesting that they were to be chained in the library which confirms that chaining was the practice long before the invention of printing in England.

William Lyndwood, Bishop of St David's and author of the *Provinciale*, by his will of 1443 directed that a chained copy of the book should be kept in the chapel of St Stephen, Westminster Abbey.

Many cathedrals and greater churches have large libraries, the most extensive being at Hereford where the cathedral library has approximately 2,000 volumes of which some 1,500 are chained. All Saints church, Hereford, also has a library of 328 volumes which are very cunningly chained. Other large libraries with chained books may be found at Wimborne Minster, Dorset; Cartmel Priory, Lancashire, and Grantham, Lincolnshire, but there are quite a few more to be found.

In 1536 the Injunctions of Henry VIII ordered that a Latin and an English Bible were to be placed in the choir of every church where they could be freely read by the people. Little appears to have been done, however, and the order was repeated in 1537, 1547 and 1559.

GLASTONBURY,
SOMERSET.
Chained books, Erasmus
'Paraphrases of the New
Testament', 1548, and a
'Breeches' Bible, 1584.

FAIRFORD,
GLOUCESTERSHIRE.
Chained 'Matthews'
Bible, 1551, on lectern
which has original C12
feet in form of beastheads.

William Tyndale, a strong supporter of the movement for reform in the Church was determined to translate the Bible into English in order that it might be available to, 'a boy that driveth the plough'. Copies arrived in this country in 1526, the printing having been carried out at Worms, Germany, but the work was given a hostile reception by the Church. One of the chief reasons for the hostility was the amount of comment and highly controversial footnotes. Miles Coverdale, who was chief translator in England, had probably worked with Tyndale and although not a profound scholar he had, like Cranmer, a good ear for prose. Coverdale began a revision of Tyndale's Bible under the patronage of Thomas Cromwell and later, after the fall of Cromwell, under Cranmer. This work, produced in 1538, became known as The Great Bible and contained a Prologue contributed by Cranmer. In time it was copies of this Bible, based on the work of Tyndale and Coverdale, which found their way into the churches, not for use during divine service but for the use of the people and so Tyndale's hopes and prayers were answered. In Lincoln Cathedral there is an ancient desk and chain in the library which was probably used for the People's Bible.

Within a few months of the accession of Edward VI in 1547, the first set of Royal Injunctions ordered every church to 'provide within three months one Boke of the whole Bible of largest volume in English and within one twelve-month the Paraphrases of Erasmus the same to be sette up in some convenient place within the church'. In addition Cranmer's first Book of Homilies was also provided. The intention behind the Injunctions was to discourage superstition and promote sound learning as the Paraphrases were commentaries upon the Gospels and the Homilies were a collection of twelve sermons on the Scriptures. This Injunction also gave considerable impetus to the chaining of books in churches. The translation of the Injunction may still be seen in a few churches, for example, Kingsthorpe, Northamptonshire, and Tavistock, Devon. By Article 6 of the Injunctions of Elizabeth I, 1559, the 1547 Injunctions were reiterated with the additional words, 'where the parishioners may well commodiously resort and read the same out of the time of common service'.

Later in 1563 Convocation issued a Second Book of Homilies and in the same year it was decreed that a translation of Foxe's *Book of Martyrs* be purchased by the wardens of every parish. This work, which was first published in English in 1563 in a huge folio known as *The Acts and Monuments of these latter and Perilous Days*, but which is known as *Foxe's Book of Martyrs*, is a graphic and controversial account of those who suffered in the cause of Protestantism.

It was widely read, four editions being printed during his lifetime and was probably ranked next to the Bible by the English Puritans. The book helped to shape popular opinion about Roman Catholicism well into the seventeenth century with its references to the evil and cruelty attributable to 'the Romische Prelates' and the description of the Spanish Inquisition. It also dealt with the martyrdom of English Protestants from the fourteenth century through the reign of Queen Mary into Foxe's own time.

To these books were also added Bishop Jewel's *Apology* (1562), and the *Defence of the Apology* (1570), for the English Church. The Canons of 1571 refer to the provision of 'the Holy Bible in the largest volume if it may conveniently be such as were lately imprinted at London'. This was the 'Bishop's Bible' revised under Archbishop Parker's auspices and published in 1568. Jewel's works, either chained or showing traces of a chain, may still be found, for example, at Chedworth, Gloucestershire; Hatfield, South Yorkshire; Kidder-

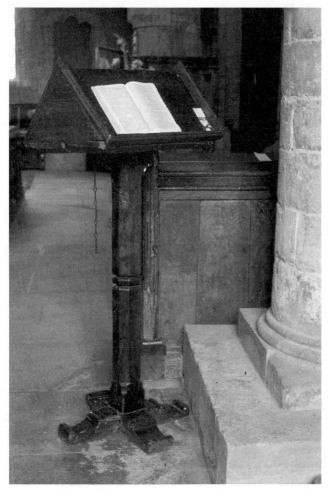

TREDINGTON,
WARWICKSHIRE.
C15 wooden lectern
showing chains.

minster, Hereford & Worcester; Lingfield, Surrey (and Bible); Newport Pagnall, Buckinghamshire; Wiggenhall St Mary, Norfolk (and Bible, Foxe and Homilies); and Wooten-Wawen, Warwickshire.

Monasteries were the chief homes of English books in medieval times and the destruction or dispersion of their libraries following their dissolution was a grievous blow to literary culture. Fortunately the custom of keeping books and manuscripts, other than service books, in cathedrals and parish churches began long before the monasteries were dissolved. Belinus Nansmoen, a wealthy Bristol merchant, bequeathed in 1416 to the church of St Mary Redcliffe, Bristol, Avon, the *Sixth Book of Decretals* and the *Constitutions of Pope Clement V* which were to be retained so that the vicar and chaplains could study them at their leisure. There can be little doubt that these books were chained.

The following is a list of old books, some chained, as well as more important church libraries taken from those set out in the reprint (1937) edition of 'English Church Furniture' by J.C. Cox and A. Harvey together with a few additions.

Abingdon, Berkshire	Bible (1611) and others.
Appleby, Cumbria	Foxe in three volumes.
Backford, Cheshire	Chained Bible (1617).
Barchester, Warwickshire	Erasmus and others with chains.
Borden, Kent	Foxe.
Bowness-on-Windermere, Cumbria	Erasmus, Jewel (1609) and Homilies.
Bridlington, Humberside	Jewel (1611) and others.
Bromsgrove, Hereford & Worcester	Jewel (1609) chained.
Canterbury Cathedral, Kent	Bible, chained.
Cartmel, Cumbria	Various literary rarities.
Cavendish, Suffolk	Early C16 two-sided wooden lectern with chained copies of Book of Homilies and Paraphrases of Erasmus.
Dronfield, Derbyshire	Jewel (1569). Chain attached to cover.
Fairford, Gloucestershire	Erasmus. Traces of chain. Lectern with chained early edition of *Institutes* and *Whole Duty of Man*.
Grantham, Lincolnshire	Library founded 1598 of 368

	books, 74 chained. Housed in room over south porch.
Hatfield, South Yorkshire	Jewel, chained.
Hatfield Broad Oak, Essex	Library of books given to the church in 1680 including Matthew Prior's poems, an Aldine Aristotle of 1498, a Vinegar Bible and rare theological books.
Kingsthorpe, Northants	Chained books comprising Erasmus (1547), Jewel (1609) and three volumes of Foxe (1641).
Kingston, Somerset	Bible (1617)
Leyland, Lancashire	Foxe, Jewel and others, chained.
Little Petherick, Cornwall	Foxe in three volumes, chained.
Luton, Bedfordshire	Bible and Foxe.
Mancetter, Warwickshire	Erasmus, Foxe and Jewel.
Newport Pagnall, Buckinghamshire	Jewel and Foxe, chained.
Stratford-upon-Avon, Warwickshire	Bible (1611).
Tavistock, Devon	Erasmus (1548), Jewel (1560).
Towcester, Northamptonshire	Chained Bibles, Homilies and Foxe.
Whitchurch, Shropshire	Foxe (1566), chained.
Wiggenhall St Mary, Norfolk	Bible, Foxe, Jewel and Homilies, chained.
York Minster, North Yorkshire	Bible (1611).

Lighting

The medieval churches of England were lighted artificially in two ways, by lamp and by candle. Most services were held, where possible, during daylight hours, except for early winter masses, as artificial lights in churches would be few and far between. Guilds usually attended the late first evensong of festivals when special provision was made for lighting. In the monastic, collegiate and greater churches where night offices were kept, the light of the sanctuary lamp before the high altar, in honour of the Blessed Sacrament, would give a dim glimmer. This lamp is frequently referred to in charters, inventories and church accounts from the thirteenth to the sixteenth centuries. There were also usually two candle sockets on the great lectern in the centre of the chancel which was used to hold the Grail (or Gradual) and the Antiphon. These were types of service books, the Grail containing responses to verses of the Psalms or text which was customarily sung by one or two cantors and the Antiphon which included texts taken from the Psalms or canticles for use in the ancient practice of antiphonal or plainsong singing. The masses had their own lights and the great festivals, Christmas, Candlemass and Easter had their special illuminations.

The lamps were cups filled with oil and containing a floating wick. As time went on, lamps, except sanctuary lamps, gave way to candles as they were found to give a better and steadier light and were more easily controlled.

In smaller churches waxed rushlights were used grouped together on a wrought-iron holder either suspended or held in sockets affixed to bench-ends or round a side altar. The rushes were picked in late summer, soaked in water, laid on the grass to bleach and then dried in the sun. They were then dipped in scalding wax in a mould. A rushlight burned for about half an hour. These moulds may still be found in churches chiselled out of a piece of stone which may form a window sill or the priest's step of a font as at White Roding, Essex. A good example of a rushlight holder may be seen at Warnham, Sussex. The pith from peeled rushes was used to make wicks for lamps or candles.

A further form of lighting mostly used in monasteries and the greater churches was the cresset or mortar which was formed of cups hollowed in stone and filled with grease or oil with a floating wick. These cresset stones were placed near doorways, or staircases, cloister corners and in dormitories. The number

THAXTED, ESSEX.
Gilded high altar hanging
sanctuary lamp.

WHITE RODING, ESSEX.
Taper moulds.

of depressions seems to vary between four and sixteen but the cresset stone at Brecon Cathedral is unique, having thirty cups. Lewannick, Cornwall, has an unusual cresset stone which is made from a circular block of granite eighteen and a half inches across on the upper surface and fifteen and three-eighths inches on the lower and being eight inches thick. There are seven cups, six being arranged around a central cup. This interesting cresset stone stands on an octagonal stand constructed of similar stone to the cresset. This stand is thirteen and a half inches in height and fourteen inches wide and has stop-chamfers on alternate faces. Wool church, Dorset has a cresset stone made from Purbeck marble which has four circular depressions.

Next to the sacrament light the most important were those which burned before the Rood. At festival times, in special devotion to the Rood, it was customary to use the Rood beam of the loft, which was sometimes known as the candle-beam, to support lights to light up the Rood. Sometimes the lights were tapers, set on prickets in the middle of copper, latten or pewter bowls, to catch the wax drippings and were maintained by regular parish funds if they were not provided for by individual benefactors or guilds. They were fixed on to the Rood beam or along the top of the parapet of the Rood loft. There

BLACKMORE, ESSEX.
C14 cresset stone.

was no specific number, sometimes only two or three and in other cases many more as at Cranbrook, Kent, where in 1509 there were no less than forty-one in use.

There was a variety of different kinds of lights used to hang before the Rood, such as lamps, branches, candelabra and long wax candles rolled into coils called 'trendles' or 'trendylls' from the middle English word 'trenden' – to roll.

All such lights were suspended by cords or chains from the roof near the east end of the nave. The pulley-wheels over which the cord or chain passed for raising or lowering the Rood light may occasionally still be found as at East Hagbourne, Oxfordshire; St Mary's, Stamford, Lincolnshire and St Peter Mancroft, Norwich, Norfolk. Henry VIII's Injunctions of 1538 prohibited all candles, tapers etc. burning before images but exempted 'the light that commonly goeth across the church by the Rood loft' and allowed it to remain. These Rood lights, however, became extinct when the Roods themselves were abolished in the sixteenth century.

The branches were iron brackets having prickets to hold tapers or candles and two very fine specimens, believed to date from the fifteenth century may be seen at Rowlstone, Hereford and Worcester. The cresting on one of the brackets has cocks and fleur-de-lis heads in honour of St Peter, the patron saint of the church and the other has swans and fleur-de-lis heads. These two brackets are unique in England.

In addition to the rows of lights along the candle-beam there was usually a special light, which was sometimes a lamp or a giant candle or taper, immediately in front of the Rood which burnt perpetually or at special times. People left bequests for the provision of wax for a taper to be burnt at a special time.

In a number of churches the chief light suspended before the Rood was a corona of lights which were usually known as 'rowells'. It took the form of a circle or wheel containing twelve to twenty candles or tapers held in bowls around the wheel. In 1494, Jane Taillour bequeathed wax to make tapers for the '12 lights burning afore the roode in ye rowelle' in the church of Blyford, Suffolk. A copy of one of these corona may be seen in the Saxon church at Chickney, Essex.

Candelabra are perhaps the most beautiful of the church lights. The oldest now extant is at Bristol Cathedral. It is made of latten and is approximately three feet in height with twelve branches arranged on two tiers, the lower one of eight and the upper one of four. The branches are gracefully curved and foliated with square-leaf decoration terminating in candle sconces. These branches spring from two globes which are held together by slender uprights, forming a sort of cage, in which is a beautiful statuette of St George and the

ROWLSTONE, HEREFORD &
WORCESTER.
C15 Candle bracket 4ft 7in
(1.397m).

CHICKNEY, ESSEX.
Copy rowell containing 20
candles.

Dragon over which there is the upper globe with pedestal on which stands another statuette of the Holy Mother, crowned and holding the Holy Child in her arms. The lower globe terminates in a grotesque animal head with a large ring through its mouth. The ring is to facilitate drawing down the chandelier for lighting and cleaning. It is of fine workmanship and is dated about the end of the fourteenth century.

Wales possesses two brass candelabra of a similar nature to the one in Bristol Cathedral. They are both of the first quarter of the sixteenth century and so of pre-Reformation date. The first is at Llanarmon-yr-lal, Clwyd, which also has a statuette of the Virgin between two tiers of branches. This candelabra is said to have been brought from the Abbey of Valle Crucia, Clwyd, at the time of its destruction. A further brass candelabra, but rather smaller, is in the village church of Llandegla, Clwyd, and has the figure of the Virgin resting upon the upper tier of branches and is easier to see. Good illustrations of these two candelabra may be seen in the 4th volume of the *Inventories* issued by the Royal Commission on the Ancient Monuments of Wales (1914). Another example of a candelabra of late medieval date may be seen at Lew Trenchard, Devon, and which has eighteen branches surmounted by a dove.

The use of branched candelabra did not die out with the Reformation. Those of the seventeenth and eighteenth centuries are mostly of brass of Flemish design and in many cases of Flemish workmanship, although some are the work of local craftsmen from Bristol or provincial workshops. These candelabra frequently have two tiers of branched candlesticks and sometimes three, on rounded stems which spring from a central globe. Others have only one tier of branched candlesticks.

The earlier types of chandelier are the more elegant, the latter being more ornate. The earlier types have a large ball below the lights which is usually polished to reflect the candles. The sconces spring from the shaft at a higher level and where there are two tiers this is repeated. The circular trays beneath the candle-holders were at first large and shallow but later became cup-like. The designs are in great variety and many of them are graceful and beautiful. The shaft is usually composed of separate pieces held together by a central rod of iron which finishes at the top with a split pin inside a loop and below with a brass knob or ring. The finials are decorated with doves or, later, with flaming torches. The sconces were cast and could be interchanged for other patterns. As the candelabra resembled the radiating legs of a common household insect they were known as 'spiders'. Candelabra were costly items and so were usually the gift of a private benefactor, the name of the donor and date generally being shown on the central globe.

At the beginning of the eighteenth century it became the fashion to light

English churches with well-designed chandeliers of brass having two tiers or even three tiers of branches springing from the shaft, a finial of perhaps a dove and a pendant to finish at the bottom. English designs of the seventeenth century are plainer than those that came from Holland at this time. During the eighteenth century the arms became shorter, drooped less and were fitted to the circumference of the spheres (globe collar) which itself became flatter. The branches became more elaborate, often hexagonal or octagonal in section and covered with scrolling. The spaces between branches and tiers were filled with ornament. The Flemish candelabra, at this period, were without finial or ornament and the branches were attached by tenons and pins, instead of hooks, to hollow trays. Manufacture of English candelabra ceased during the nineteenth century.

Unfortunately many of these beautiful candelabra fell victims to church restorers who, in their ignorance, ejected everything not purely Gothic! Mr J. Charles Cox in his book, *English Church Fittings, Furniture and Accessories* (1923), cites the case where would-be restorers of the church at Gedling, Nottinghamshire in 1890 actually mutilated three seventeenth century chandeliers, twisting them up to make a singularly tasteless lectern!

St Mary Redcliffe, Bristol, used to be lighted by candelabra but only one of the originals now remains dated 1650. This was used as a model for the reproduction of a new series which were placed throughout the aisles.

The church at Wedmore, Somerset, originally had a very handsome brass candelabra hanging from the centre of the nave in solitary splendour. The inscription read, 'The generous gift of Mr John Tucker of Blackford, in this parish in 1779'. In 1854 Miss Ann Redman added two more modelled on the same pattern, the first of which is inscribed, 'The generous gift of Miss Ann Redman of Wedmore, 1854. Thomas Hall & Co., fecit, Bristol'. The second one repeats the donor's name and date.

In the parish church of St John the Baptist, Cirencester, Gloucestershire, there is a pair of brass chandeliers (1701) by John Spooner of Bristol. The branches, which have the combination of human heads and fish heads, are similar to those of the chandelier shown in Vermeer's *A Painter in his Studio*, which dates from *c.*1666.

Hatfield Broad Oak church, Essex, has a very fine brass eighteenth century chandelier with thirty-six ornamental branches. Axbridge, Somerset, also has a fine brass chandelier of three tiers. It was bought in Bristol in 1729 for £14 5s 0d and weighs 1cwt 2qtr 17lb. At Winchcombe, Gloucestershire, there is a two-tier chandelier of local work based on London designs having a gilded angel finial surmounted with a wrought-iron Greek cross with fine scroll-work in each quarter to which is attached the chain from which the chandelier is suspended.

Candle-holders of various kinds are to be found in many churches. They differ from mere holes in the top of a bench-end, or choir desk, to tall wooden holders at the ends of the seventeenth century pews in the north aisle of Kilburn church, North Yorkshire and the brass bracket holders to be found on lecterns, pulpits or box pews. Processional torch or bier lights may also be found made in polished brass having a removable four-sided incurving and tapering base on four bun feet, a cylindrical stem with two stepped knots and a drip pan of similar shape to the base with plain cylindrical socket for the candle.

Later in the eighteenth and nineteenth centuries oil lamps were used followed by gas and electricity. I believe Tetbury, Gloucestershire, is still lit by gas. Even today some of our country churches are lit by oil lamps as at Norton Mandeville, Essex, and Bradfield and Barton Turf, Norfolk.

Altar candlesticks came into general use about the beginning of the thirteenth century. They were usually in pairs and made of latten, copper-gilt or of silver. The usual number was two and those that remain are usually found in pairs. The earliest and most beautiful examples are preserved in St Thomas's, Bristol, which date from early in the thirteenth century. Although their origin of production has not been established it is possible that they are of British craftsmanship.

There are two pairs, the smaller being five and a half inches in height and the larger ten and a half inches, both pairs resembling each other except that the smaller one contains less decoration and has only one knot on the stem instead of three. They are made of copper, originally gilt and encrusted with Champlevé enamel (i.e. enamelling done by cutting out troughs from the metal and filling them with coloured enamel), much of which has been lost. The candlesticks have a spreading, triangular, pyramidal base, slender shaft with globular knots, one and three respectively and a flat drip-pan head. Subsequent to their manufacture sconces of latten have been added. The decoration is Romanesque with geometrical figures, scrolls and monsters.

Many of the cathedral churches and collegiate chapels in England have fine examples of silversmiths' art in altar candlesticks of post-Reformation times. Canterbury has a silver-gilt candlestick, probably one of a pair, which is seventeen and a half inches in height, excluding the pricket, and is early sixteenth century. Rochester, Kent has a silver altar candlestick hallmarked 1653 and York Minster has two silver altar candlesticks hallmarked 1672–3. They weigh fifty-three ounces and are plain circular silver-gilt. They were given by Lord Beaumont. Norwich Cathedral has altar candlesticks standing twenty and a half inches in height, date-marked 1663. They are inscribed, 'Ad Sacros Usus Ecesiae Cathedralis Sanctae Et Individuae Trinitatis Norwici

WINCHCOMBE,
GLOUCESTERSHIRE.
Very fine candelabra *c.*1753.
Local work using London
designs.

KILBURN, NORTH
YORKSHIRE.
C17 wooden pew candle
holder.

BRADFIELD, NORFOLK.
Oil lamp.

BRITISH MUSEUM, LONDON.
C14 Limoges ware altar
candlesticks. Centre C13
(1220–1230): Right *c.*1230: Left
C14 (early).

Donavit Civitas Norwicensis' which roughly translated reads, 'Consecrated to the Cathedral Church and Holy Indivisible Trinity Norwich Gift of the Community of the capital city of the Diocese of Norwich'.

Mention must be made of the oldest and most remarkable church candlestick in England. It is probably one of a pair of altar candlesticks of the early twelfth century, *c*.1110 made of gilt bell-metal and now in the Victoria and Albert Museum. Formerly it was in the abbey church of St Peter, Gloucester (later to become Gloucester Cathedral) where the donor, Abbot Peter ruled between 1107 and 1113. The candlestick is twenty-three inches in height with three dragons' heads for feet and the whole is ornamented with pierced foliage, figures and monsters in relief. On the top is a pricket bowl which has an inscription around the outside rim and on a ribbon which runs round the shaft it is recorded that the candlestick was given by Abbot Peter to the Holy Church of St Peter, Gloucester. A further inscription, later than the candlestick, is on the inside of the pricket bowl and records that it was a gift to the church of Le Mans by Thomas de Poche.

12

Chantries and Chantry Chapels

Every religious house that was founded in this country from the eighth to the thirteenth century owed its foundation to a royal benefactor or to a wealthy landowner.

Following the Norman Conquest the barons and their successors eagerly associated themselves with the founding of monasteries throughout the land. These monasteries soon became rich and powerful through the continued patronage of the rich and great who were fully aware of the dignity which was thus conferred on their families. They were also aware of the spiritual advantages of the prayers which the brethren would offer up on their behalf as these prayers, or intercessions, offered regularly by the brethren, were one of the main conditions laid down by the benefactor and their lands and property were held accordingly. The religious houses were, therefore, under legal obligations to carry out their founders' wishes. The less wealthy, who did not have the means to found a religious house, also wished to have prayers offered for themselves and their families. Their wishes were expressed in benefactions, according to their means, to a convent or church and these secured for the donors certain privileges, which included the prayers of the brethren.

From Saxon days the laity often desired to be associated with the family of the abbeys. They were known as 'confraters' and reference to them may often be found in monastic records. They paid for this privilege by paying in things temporal for spiritual benefits which they hoped they would receive.

From the king downward men and women of all classes associated themselves with the religious houses. King Canute and his brother Harold were received into the 'family' of Christ Church, Canterbury, the King marking the occasion by presenting a copy of the Gospels to the convent. This copy is now in the British Museum.

A roll of benefactors and confraters was kept in every religious house and the brethren offered up prayers for their well-being whilst alive and for their souls after death. Whenever the building or enlargement of a religious house was required the roll served as a list of subscribers which also included the names of donors of gifts in kind. In the early thirteenth century, an increasing veneration for Our Lady led to the building, rebuilding or enlargement of

Lady Chapels. At Westminster Abbey there was substituted for the Confessor's easternmost chapel a large Lady Chapel. It was begun by Abbot Hamez and finished by Abbot Berking who was buried in front of its High Altar. It was consecrated in 1220. The money was largely raised by subscriptions entitling the donors to indulgence in purgatory. An indulgence was the remission in part or in full of the pain that sinful souls would suffer as penance in purgatory. The medieval Church optimistically assumed that most Christians would not go to Hell but, at the same time, did not assume that they would go directly to Heaven. They would, instead, go to an intermediate place called purgatory, a state in which souls of those who had died in grace must atone venial sins. These were sins, which though evil, did not totally estrange the soul from God's grace, unlike mortal sin. The conviction that sinners suffered in the afterlife but could be helped by the living was firmly held and vigorously acted upon.

It was believed that the sufferings of the souls of the dead were very intense and could last for a long time. The living often sought to ease the pains of their departed relatives and to help them on their way to Heaven. This they believed they could do because, as Christians, they could pray for one another and God would hear them. Mary and other saints were asked to pray to God on behalf of the living and this belief in the power of the saints' intercession formed the theological basis for the firmly-rooted cult of the saints. If the saints could pray for the living then it followed that the living could pray for the dead in purgatory.

There were many ways to help the dead, including almsgiving, fasting, pilgrimage and prayer but it was the Mass which was regarded as the most perfect form of prayer because it re-enacted Christ's atoning sacrifice to his Father and was thought, therefore, to be the best way to help those in purgatory. Many people made arrangements for Masses while living or in their wills. If arrangements had not been made by the deceased his family was under a strong moral obligation to make the necessary provision. The usual arrangement was for a Mass on the day of the burial, a Mass on the month's anniversary of the burial and then on the year's anniversary.

In addition to the roll of benefactors and confraters kept by the religious houses there was also a parochial bede (prayer) roll kept by the parish churches of all benefactors for whose souls the prayers of the parishioners were desired. The bede roll was placed on the High Altar during the celebration of Mass on Sundays and festivals when the names were read aloud by the priest to the worshippers. That the parishioners were eager to be included in the roll and to be prayed for is shown by the many references to the roll in medieval wills. An early reference in 1246 is of a London cordwainer (shoemaker), Algrand, who granted a piece of land to the church of St Augustine by St Paul's Cathedral for the enlargement of the church and to include an altar dedicated to Our Lady. In acknowledgement of the gift he, his wife Rose and his first wife, Alice, were to be made 'participants in all the benefits and prayers which should be made in that church for ever'. His name was to be added to the bede roll and a special prayer said for his soul in all the Masses sung at the altar which he had founded. It would seem that prayers for the souls of the dead were sometimes said from the rood loft as Thomas Jonys of Bristol by his will of 1464 directed that the souls of his wife and himself be recommended to the prayers of the parishioners of St Nicholas' church 'in pulpito', i.e. from the Rood loft. Original bede rolls are still to be found as, for example, at St Mary's Church, Sandwich, Kent, where not only the names are recorded but also the various gifts are enumerated and also at St Michael's Cornhill, London. Durham Cathedral had 'an excellent fine book' containing the names of all the benefactors of St Cuthbert's Church, from the time of its foundation and which was kept on the High Altar. This register is a richly bound volume although now shorn of its gold and silver binding and is now in the British Museum together with a similar record from St Alban's Abbey.

Towards the close of the thirteenth century the piety which had expressed itself in the founding of religious houses was directed towards the more personal endowments which we know as chantries which supported a priest who, on the death of the founder, said Mass for his soul, provision often being made in money or in kind for further Masses to be recited periodically and on the anniversary. When Queen Eleanor of Castile, the wife of Edward I died in 1290 at Harby, Nottinghamshire, the King went to Archbishop John le Romayne of York desiring the prayers of the faithful for her soul and the Archbishop immediately granted an indulgence of forty days to those who responded. Provision was made for perpetual services to her memory and the repose of her soul, not only at the places where her body rested on its way to Westminster and which were later marked by Eleanor crosses, but in almost every part of the kingdom. At Harby a perpetual chantry was founded for the Queen, for the endowment of which one hundred marks were granted to the Dean of Lincoln in 1292. The prebendary of North Clifton was to receive ten marks a year out of which he was to pay one hundred shillings to the chantry priest and to find him a lodging and also to provide furniture for the altar. The King founded other similar chantries but the greatest was the one at Westminster Abbey, the final resting place of Eleanor. The King was profuse in his gifts to the Abbey monks that the commemoration might be both splendid and perpetual. The gifts included no less than twenty-two manors in the counties of Essex, Kent, Buckinghamshire, Warwickshire and Middlesex.

The annual observance in the Abbey, at which all the nobility and bishops were expected to attend, began on St Andrew's eve (November 29th) when one hundred wax candles, each weighing twelve pounds, continued to burn until high Mass on the following day. All the bells of the Abbey were rung incessantly and divine offices were chanted unceasingly. Daily, during the whole year, thirty massive tapers of wax remained on Eleanor's tomb. They were lighted on great festivals but at other times only two were kept constantly burning day and night. At the end of the commemoration gifts of money were distributed to the poor and to the friars and hospitallers of many London establishments. Every abbot at Westminster was bound by oath to observe religiously and scrupulously the whole of the ceremonies which continued for two and a half centuries until the Reformation, when the money which enabled the ceremonies to take place and the candles to be kept alight, was confiscated.

The Chantry

A chantry was literally a mass recited at an altar for the well-being and good estate of the founder during his lifetime and for the repose of his soul after death. In addition it kept the name of the founder and his family fresh in the memory of succeeding generations, particularly when a special chantry chapel was erected for the recitation of Masses.

Perhaps the most distinctive development in parochial life in the fourteenth and fifteenth centuries was the growth of chantries. As men's confidence in the monastic orders began to wane their benefactions were transferred to the foundation of chantries or endowment of priests to say daily Masses for the souls of the benefactors and their families. By the fifteenth century all the larger churches contained a number of such chantries, often signified by a separate altar or chantry-chapel which might be built on and sometimes housed the tomb of the founder, or part of the church might be screened off to form a chapel, and there were probably few parish churches in England without such a foundation.

Evidence may often be seen in parish churches at the east ends of side aisles, or where there were no aisles in the two eastern corners of the nave, where a piscina may be found proving that, originally, there was an altar nearby which was used by a chantry priest. Piscinas, other than in the chancel, may be found in other parts of the church, especially on the north and south walls of the nave indicating that there was probably an altar used by a chantry priest. Occasionally chantries were founded at an altar standing against the Rood screen, which in a greater church was frequently a stone structure spanning the nave at the east end and was of sufficient depth to enable altars to be placed on either side of the door opening into the choir. Examples of Rood screen altars may be seen at Patricio, Brecon, Powys, where altars are placed on both sides of the screen entrance and St David's Cathedral, Dyfed, where an altar is placed on the north side of the entrance to the stone screen (pulpitum).

Altars were sometimes attached to the more important tombs at the west end of the church, especially chantry tombs and a good example of this may be seen at the chantry tomb of Henry Lord Marney at Layer Marney, Essex.

In chantry foundations of persons of rank and wealth the endowment often provided for the establishment of an almshouse, or hospital as it was termed. The hospital housed and maintained a number of poor men or bedesmen to whom the chantry priest, who was usually master of the hospital, served as chaplain and distributed their allowances and clothing. The bedesmen wore distinguishing apparel which was generally a long cloth gown of dark colour bearing the badge of the founder on one sleeve. They were bound by the duties laid down by the founder and were under obligation to attend church

LAYER MARNEY, ESSEX.
C16 tomb chest, Lord John Marney with chantry altar in background.

daily, to pray for the soul of their benefactor and were required to kneel at
his tomb and make their supplications with the priest. The number of bedesmen
in a hospital varied from five to thirteen.

To ensure that the duties of the bedesmen were strictly observed a precise
ceremony was frequently prepared by the founder and it is interesting to read
the ceremonial required of bedesmen by Henry Lord Marney (d. 1523). The
following is an extract:

> such as shall say at least their paternoster, ave and creed in Latin ... at their
> uprising they shall say for the souls of Sir Robert Marney, Knt. and his wife
> and all my children, five paternosters, five aves and one creed and every day
> go to the church of Layer Marney, and there hear Mass in the new chapel.
> Moreover, I will that at his first coming into the church, everyone of them
> shall kneel down before the Sacrament and say a paternoster and an ave, and
> then go to my tomb and there, kneling down, say for my soul and for the other
> souls above named three paternosters, three aves and one creed in worship of
> the Trinity; and then go down into the church and there in the time of Mass
> or else before their departure ... say for the above-named souls, Our Lady's
> Psalter [i.e. the Rosary] and at night-time before their going to bed, every one
> of them to say kneeling on their knees five paternosters, five aves and the creed
> for the souls aforesaid. Also I will that such of them as can say De Profundis
> [Psalm 130] shall say it in lieu of the paternosters etc. Also that every Wednesday
> and Friday they shall go into the church at afternoon and there kneeling about
> my tomb say for my soul and souls aforesaid Our Lady's Psalter; and if any of
> them can say Dirige [Office for the dead], I will that they say it in lieu of Our
> Lady's Psalter.

The nature of a chantry depended upon the value of the endowment. In the
majority of cases it was limited to perhaps one, two, three or ten years. In 1533
Robert Astbroke bequeathed a sum of money for a priest to recite soul Masses
for his soul in Wicomb church at Jesus altar for two years. Moderate endowments took the form of the recitation of Masses on the first, third, seventh and
thirtieth day after the death of the testator with an obit (a Mass sung on the
anniversary of the death) once a year or perhaps a trental of masses which was
a daily Mass for a month after the testator's decease.

Obits were very popular as the endowment was less costly than a chantry.
The payment for an obit was usually made to the parish priest who would be
responsible for the observance of the rite and also for the distribution of alms
to the poor out of the payment. Most obits provided for alms which usually
amounted to half of the bequest and which were used for charitable purposes.
The use of candles at an obit was an important part of the procedure. On the
eve of the obit a black pall was thrown over the tomb of the founder and a

WRITTLE, ESSEX.
'Carpenter' chantry chapel. Endowed by Wm.
Carpenter d. 1526.

BURFORD, OXFORDSHIRE.
C15 St Peter's chantry chapel.
After Suppression preserved as
family pew of Lord of the
Manor (*c.*1580–1875).

157

candle placed at the head and another at the foot where they were left to burn until the following day when four other candles were lighted and remained burning until high Mass had been sung for his soul. The four candles were then extinguished and two others placed there until after Compline, the last office of the day. Where there was no tomb a hearse was set up west of the altar and covered with a black pall.

The founding and endowment of a perpetual chantry in the fifteenth and sixteenth centuries was very costly and could only be entertained by the wealthy. It made provision for Masses to be recited for ever and frequently included the erection of a special chapel which was reserved solely for the soul-Masses of the founder and family. Within the chapel an altar was set up at which the Masses were celebrated.

These chantry chapels were sometimes additional chapels built on to the main body of the church, such as those at Ely (Bishop Alcock's chantry); the magnificent chapel at Windsor (Cardinal Beaufort's chantry); and the beautiful Beauchamp chapel at St Mary's church, Warwick. In the parish churches there are many examples of chantry chapels which have been added to the main building, e.g. Burford, Oxfordshire which has fifteenth-century chapels, such as St Katherine's opening off the north transept and Holy Trinity off the south transept and the Carpenter chapel in Writtle church, Essex. The majority are very much smaller and usually comprise a gilded and painted rectangular screenwork within the building, of stone, wood or metal, perhaps surmounted by crested cornices or gables. They were mostly roofed with small-scale fan vaulting of great beauty and were graceful little buildings within buildings. Some fine examples of these small, elegant, box-like chapels may be found at Wells Cathedral, Somerset (Dean Sugar's chantry); Winchester Cathedral, Hampshire (Bishop Gardiner's chantry); Tewkesbury Abbey, Gloucestershire (Beauchamp chantry, Dispenser chantry); and Burford, Oxfordshire (St Peter's chantry).

Following the Black Death (1349), the number of foundations rapidly increased and together with the associated increase in prayers the horrors of the frightful mortality remained long in peoples' memories. The trauma caused by the pestilence served to concentrate men's thoughts on the uncertainty of life and with recurring outbreaks turned their thoughts to the next world, so that during the second half of the century the provision of soul-Masses multiplied considerably.

Of the two thousand or more chantries existing at the time of the Suppression, the great majority had been founded during the fifteenth century and by the sixteenth century the chantry system had become vast indeed. At the lesser altars in cathedral, monastic and many parish churches there was an increasing recitation of soul-Masses every morning. As already stated only the wealthy –

TEWKESBURY ABBEY, GLOUCESTERSHIRE.
Fitzhamon chantry chapel *c.*1397. Enriched with fan vaulting, tracery and original tiles showing Fitzhamon Arms.

royalty, nobles, bishops, abbots, merchant princes and similar classes of people were able to include a special oratory as part of a chantry foundation as well as providing a stipend for a priest to sing the Masses for the founder and 'all the faithful departed'. The chantry priest often carried out other duties such

TEWKESBURY ABBEY, GLOUCESTERSHIRE. Warwick Chantry Chapel *c.*1397. Two storeys with fan vaulted roofs. Erected by Lady Isabella de Spenser, Countess of Warwick.

as assisting the parish priest in the normal offices in the church or teaching in a free school.

In some places a college might be set up, a form of community and rule to which the chantry priests had to adhere, the parish church to which it was attached being termed 'collegiate'. The effect of this was that as the church was in dual use special arrangements had to be made for the services and the times at which they were held. There were two ways in which this could be carried out. One was to divide the building into two parts by enlarging the chancel and reserve it for chantry Masses and transfer the parish altar to the nave as had already happened in monastic churches. The alternative way was for the chantry and parish priests to share the building as it stood and endeavour to come to some agreement over the timetable. As can be imagined the chantry priests were not popular with the incumbents of the churches they were using nor with most of the parishioners who were of the opinion that they had not enough to do.

Despite this, new chantries continued to be founded right up to the early years of the sixteenth century. The early chantries mostly had individual benefactors but later either ordinary parishioners combined to meet the expenses of a foundation, or a trade, religious guild or fraternity. The religious guilds were established for purposes of mutual benefit, works of piety and charity and for the celebration of Masses on behalf of the brethren, living and dead. In effect they were benefit societies and burial clubs and each guild was known by the name of its patron saint. A very popular dedication was Corpus Christi, the celebration of the Feast being marked by a solemn procession of the Blessed Sacrament and a display of pageantry by the members of the guild.

The trade guilds had as the special object of their existence the protection of some kind of work, trade or handicraft, e.g. cutlers, wool merchants, tailors, smiths, butchers, brewers, dyers, bakers, mariners and other, which testified to the importance of trade and industry. The religious and trade guilds were virtually chantry foundations and from the fifteenth century built their own chapels in the parish churches. The maintenance and the enlargement of many town churches were due largely to the munificence of the guilds. The magnificent south porch of Cirencester Church, Gloucestershire, is a monument to the trade guilds whose brethren met in the upper chambers to transact business. Nor did they lack in social activities; they had their feasts and pageants and drama in the form of 'mystery' plays.

The mutual help and comfort afforded by a guild embraced the spiritual side of life and included mutual prayers for the living and the dead. The guild especially made much of the burial of its members which was conducted with great solemnity. All the members were bound to attend the funeral and provision was made for the continual offering of Masses for the welfare of the living and the repose of their departed brothers and sisters. By the rules of the Lancaster Guild, Lancashire,

> on the death of a member all the brethren then in the town shall come to placebo and dirge, if summoned by the bellman, or pay 2d. All shall go to the mass held for a dead brother or sister; each brother or sister so dying shall have at the mass on the day of burial six torches and eighteen wax-lights, and at other services two torches and four wax-lights. If any of the gild die outside Lancaster, within twenty miles, twelve brethren shall wind and deck the body at the cost of the gild and if the brother or sister so dying wished to be buried where he died the same twelve shall see that he has fitting burial there where he died.

Some of the guilds had a hearse and embroidered pall which were used at funerals of members of the guild and sometimes let out to others.

Some of the guilds were very large, not so much for mutual benefit or regulation of trade but for the foundation and conduct of enterprises for the benefit of the whole community; for promoting the glory of God and increasing the number or services and the means of grace for the population of the town; for founding a hospital or grammar school; for building and repairing bridges and highways etc. The Gild of Ludlow, Shropshire, had seven chaplains and maintained, in addition, two deacons and four choristers to sing divine service in the parish church. It also supported a grammar school, an almshouse for thirty-two poor people and gave liberal gifts to the poor. The Coventry, West Midlands, 'gild merchant' kept a lodging house and thirteen beds 'to lodge poor folk coming through the land on pilgrimage or other work of charity ... with a keeper of the house and a woman to wash the pilgrims' feet'.

Mention must be made of one of probably the oldest of houses of charity in England at St Cross, Winchester, Hampshire. It was founded in 1136 by the Conqueror's grandson, Henry of Blois, brother of King Stephen and Bishop of Winchester, for the feeding of one hundred poor men as well as housing, clothing and feeding thirteen more too old and sick to help themselves. The Bishop placed the hospital under the direction of the Knights of St John and their connection with it lasted about a hundred years. A master was appointed to look after the poor and old people each of whom was given a black cap and gown with silver Greek cross, the symbol of the Knights Hospitallers.

In the fifteenth century Cardinal Henry Beaufort gave a new lease of life to the house by founding the 'Almshouse of Noble Poverty', richly endowing it with beauty and new buildings. He built a noble tower, known as the Beaufort Tower, over the entrance courtyard, houses for two priests, three

ST CROSS HOSPITAL, WINCHESTER, HAMPSHIRE.
Entrance gateway and old dining hall.

sisters and thirty-five brethren. These brethren are distinguished from those of
the earlier foundation by gowns of a mulberry colour instead of black and
their hats have tassels.

On arrival one is greeted as pilgrims have been greeted here for eight
hundred years, with the offer of the 'Wayfarer's Dole', a piece of bread and
a drink of ale from a horn mug. Through all these centuries it has been available
to all who ask and was originally a more satisfying 'dole'. The noble Norman
and Early English church built for the poor brethren is a majestic place and a
visit to St Cross is one never to be forgotten. The charity still goes on and
the brethren in their gowns and Tudor caps continue to spend the evening of
their days in this lovely old place.

Avery Cornburgh, Esquire of the Body to Henry VI and Edward IV in the
fifteenth century, founded a charity for a priest to pray for his soul and the
souls of his friends in the chapel of St Edward, Romford, Essex, which was
rebuilt in the mid-nineteenth century and is now the parish church of St
Edward-the-Confessor. Unusual obligations were laid upon the priest who, in
addition to singing Masses for the founder was required to preach at least twice
a year in four churches in the county, viz. Hornchurch, South Ockendon,

Ingrave and South Weald as well as Romford chapel. For all these duties he received a stipend of £10 a year and a dwelling house. This chantry house or 'priest's chamber' still remains at the east end of the present church, facing the market place. It is a timber-framed building with jetties to the street and churchyard and may have formed part of a larger building which extended eastward along the market place with an open yard. The building was much altered in the eighteenth or early nineteenth century and is now known as Church House.

It frequently happened that a chantry priest would be reciting his office at an aisle altar before high Mass for the parishioners had commenced. The parish priest disapproved of this and appealed to the bishop who directed that chantry Masses should not begin until high Mass was in progress. The chantry priest claimed that, standing before his altar, he was unable to see when the parochial mass had begun. The difficulty was overcome by cutting an oblique opening or slit, known as a squint, through the wall at the side of the chancel arch which would allow the chantry priest to have a direct view of the high altar from the aisle and observe what was taking place in the chancel. Probably the most unusual squint is at Holy Trinity church, Bradford-on-Avon, Wiltshire, where there is a squint almost twenty feet long due to being cut through the walls of both nave and chancel which are not in alignment.

Towards the end of the thirteenth century the acquisition of lands by the religious foundations was increasing to such an extent that some form of control was considered necessary. Landed property owned by the Church, whether bequeathed or purchased, deprived the Crown or the feudal lords of the services belonging to such lands as well as to certain death dues. In order to overcome this deprivation the Statute of Mortmain was passed in 1279 during the reign of Edward I which forbade the alienation or transfer of lands and rents in such a way that they should come into 'dead hand'. The endowment of chantries was, therefore, affected by the statute and, as a result, before a chantry could be founded an inquiry was instituted to determine whether the king's revenue would suffer by the alienation of the property that was to provide the endowment. The sheriff of the county was directed to summon a jury to hold the inquiry and to report their findings to the Crown. If it was proved that the benefaction could be made without harm to the royal revenue because the founder would have sufficient property left to meet the Crown dues, a licence was duly granted under the Mortmain act. Once a licence had been issued and the leave of the bishop and the goodwill of the ordinary or governing body of the church had been obtained, the establishment of the chantry could be proceeded with. Failure to obtain and produce a licence when called upon might result in the seizure of the property by the Crown or the imposition of a substantial fine.

In 1342 William of Erthyngton by his will bequeathed some tenements in the parish of St Martin Outwich, Threadneedle Street, London, to the prior and convent of St Bartholomew, Smithfield, London, and directed that he should be buried in the conventional church 'if so be that they undertake to provide a chantry there for the good of my soul'. However, it was not to be. Evidently the prior had disregarded the statute, for more than thirty years later the convent was fined forty marks for failure to produce the royal licence for the alienation of the tenements. This fine was a heavy one and in the purchasing power of today could probably be about £21,000.

The parish church plan near the end of the Gothic period was largely intended to meet the devotional needs of the clergy and to provide sufficient room for a number of chantry altars. Although a church had been much enlarged and eventually looked imposing it was not always a spacious building. The tendency was to reduce the interior by dividing it into nave and chancel separated by a screen and to fill each part with chapels and fittings as well as ornamentation. The breaking up of much of the available space in the body of the church made it difficult for a really large number of people to worship together; even in the larger churches the aisles were partly filled with small screened-off spaces each with its own altar. These screens are known as parclose screens. At the suppression of the chantries parclose screens suffered the fate of the chancel rood screens but some were converted into squires pews. The general effect, despite the absence of pews, was a cluttered and crowded church.

The founding of chantries continued until the close of the reign of Henry VIII, the last being founded in 1547 at Welsh Newton, Hereford and Worcester. Many died out through inadequate endowment or due to negligence on the part of the incumbent, especially in parish churches. Large numbers of obits and anniversaries had lapsed with the passage of time and from the indifference of the priest responsible for their observance.

The suppression of chantries was inevitable. The tide of the Reformation was to sweep them away as it did the monastic establishments, shrines, relics, pilgrimages, the cult of the Virgin and much else and it was inevitable that sooner or later the parish churches would be regarded as legitimate for further plunder, in particular the chantry properties and endowments.

The first move towards their dissolution was in 1529, during the reign of Henry VIII, when Parliament passed an Act forbidding any person after Michaelmas of that year to accept any stipend for singing Masses for the dead. This was followed by another Act in 1545 which transferred the property of all chantry foundations to the Royal Exchequer 'for good and godly uses'. A

BEESTON, NORFOLK.
C14 parclose screen chapel in north aisle.

few patrons shrewdly anticipating the measures of suppression, dissolved chantries on their own account and enriched themselves by pocketing the endowment. In 1545 the Duke of Norfolk suppressed the Stonehouse chantry in East Tilbury church, Essex, the endowment of £12 5s 3d being used for the building of a blockhouse for coastal defence.

Before the 'godly uses' had been defined Henry VIII died in 1547 and the Suppression was deferred until the first year of Edward VI's reign when a further Act was passed 'whereby chantries, colleges, free chapels and the possessions of the same be given to the King's Majesty'. The reason given was that 'the doctrine and vain opinions of purgatory and masses were upholden by the abuse of trentals and masses'.

The Act of 1547 gave the Crown all the properties, rents and annuities which had furnished stipends for the chantry priests, together with the funds of the parish guilds and fraternities which had been 'assigned to superstitious objects'. 'And also be it ordained and enacted by the authority of this present Parliament, that Our Sovereign Lord, the King shall have and enjoy all such goods, chattels, jewels, plate, ornaments and other moveables as were or be the common goods of every such college, chantry, free chapel or stipendiary priest, belonging or annexed to the furniture or services of the several

BOXGROVE PRIORY, SUSSEX.
De la Warr chantry chapel, early C16. Masses for the souls of De la Warr (d. 1525) and his lady (d. 1532) were sung for a few years before the Suppression. De la Warr's son requested Thomas Cromwell to spare the abbey. Cromwell refused but allowed him to purchase the land and goods and the church was made parochial.

foundations (2 Edw. VI. c. 14)'. Under this Act, Commissioners were appointed to survey the corporation, guilds and fraternities attached to all churches up and down the land, 'thereby to know what money was bestowed to the founding or maintenance of any priest or priests, anniversary or obit or any other like thing, light or lamp by them or any of them'.

In all, 90 collegiate foundations, 110 hospitals (almshouses) and 2,374 guilds, chantries and free chapels were dissolved. A few of the chapels of ease fortunately survived the act of spoliation, for in some instances the local people purchased the endowment from the Commissioners and provided the stipend for the priest.

A church to which a chantry college was attached was still parochial; the master or warden of the college was virtually the parish priest although the cure of souls was assigned to one of the chaplains. When, therefore, a chantry college was suppressed, the parishioners regained full possession of the church to which the college had been attached. It must be said, however, that sometimes the church proved to be far larger than the parishioners required or indeed were disposed to keep in repair and so they suffered grievous mutilation, chiefly by the destruction of the choir. The collegiate church of St John, Chester, founded in the eleventh century, was the cathedral of the three dioceses of Coventry, Lichfield and Chester until the reign of Henry VIII. In 1548 in the reign of Edward VI, the King's Commissioners recommended that as the nave was sufficient for parochial purposes the lead should be stripped from the roof of the choir. Although the church was used for parish worship until 1630 the choir gradually fell into decay and was eventually demolished. The fine Norman nave, however, is still in use as a parish church.

Under the Chantries Act 1547 the ex-chantry priests were granted pensions by the Commissioners who were authorised under the Act. It is not clear as to the amounts of pensions awarded as David Knowles in his book, *Bare Ruined Choirs*, states that chantry priests could enjoy a pension of four to five pounds. G.H. Cook however, in his book, *Medieval Chantries and Chantry Chapels*, gives instances from the returns made by the Commissioners as to the amounts of pension awarded, for example, to the priests who served the altars in Carlisle Cathedral the amounts varied from £2 7s 4d, for the priest attached to the chantry of St Roch to £5 10s 0d for the one serving the altar of Our Lady. Some of the chantry priests were ex-monks, who became chantry priests following the Dissolution of the Monasteries and were, therefore, already in possession of a pension and who would now receive a second pension. It is very likely that within a few years of the surrender most of the able-bodied, worthy and less indolent priests, had found some sort of clerical occupation for themselves.

Deprived of their office and means of livelihood some chantry priests, particularly in London, found themselves subjected to insults and indignities from the general public. It is recorded that in November 1547 a proclamation was made against the evil behaviour of citizens and others towards priests who complained that they could not walk freely in the streets or attend the Court at Westminster without being reviled and having their tippets and caps violently pulled.

Perhaps the most surprising feature of the suppression of the chantries was the ease with which the more able of the religious adapted themselves to the new conditions of their changing world.

Some fine examples of chantry chapels still extant are:

Berkshire	St George's Chapel, Windsor:
	(a) The Beaufort Chapel
	(b) The Upswick Chapel
Cambridgeshire	Ely Cathedral:

	(a) Bishop Alcock's Chapel
	(b) Bishop West's Chapel

Derbyshire — Chesterfield, St Mary and All Saints:
- (a) The Foljambe Chapel
- (b) The Cotton Chapel
- (c) The St Mary Magdalen Chapel
- (d) The Holy Cross Chapel

Devon — Paignton:
The Kirkham Chantry Screen
Cullompton:
The Lane Chapel

Dorset — Christchurch:
- (a) The Salisbury Chapel
- (b) The Berkeley Chapel
- (c) Prior Draper's Chapel

Essex — East Horndon:
Two small chantry chapels two storeys high: not known by whom founded
Halstead:
Bouchier Chapel. Effigy with bedesman
Layer Marney:
North chapel – priest's chamber with unique chantry altar and Tudor chimney. Effigy of Lord John Marney on terracotta tomb without canopy: five bedesmen were to meet daily with their chaplains in the chapel for Mass for the souls of the Marneys
Writtle:
Carpenter Chantry – south aisle. There were originally four chantry chapels

Gloucestershire — Tewkesbury Abbey:
- (a) Lord Edward de Spenser Chapel
- (b) The Trinity Chapel
- (c) The Warwick Chapel
- (d) The Fitzhamon Chapel
- (e) The Beauchamp Chapel

Hampshire — Winchester Cathedral:
- (a) Bishop Fox's Chapel
- (b) Bishop William of Wykeham's Chapel

	(c) Cardinal Beaufort's Chapel
	(d) Bishop Waynflete's Chapel
	(e) Bishop Langton's Chapel
Herefordshire	Hereford Cathedral:
	Bishop Stanbury's Chapel
Kent	Canterbury Cathedral:
	(a) Chapel of the Black Prince
	(b) Henry IV's Chapel
London	Westminster Abbey:
	(a) Henry V's Chapel
	(b) Henry VII's Chapel
	(c) Abbot Islip's Chapel
Norfolk	Norwich Cathedral:
	(a) Bishop Goldwell's Chapel
	(b) Bishop Nykke's (Nix) Chapel
	(c) Bouchon Chapel
Nottinghamshire	Newark:
	(a) The Markham Chapel
	(b) The Meyning Chapel
Oxfordshire	Burford:
	(a) Timbered structured chapel with wooden canopy
	(b) The Sylvester chapel – Guild chapel of Guild of Merchants
	North Leigh:
	The Wilcote Chapel
Somerset	Well's Cathedral:
	(a) Bishop Bubwith's chapel
	(b) Dr Suger's Chapel
Sussex	Boxgrove Priory:
	Lord de le Warr's Chapel
Wiltshire	Bromham:
	(a) The Tocote Chapel
	(b) The Beauchamp Chapel
	Devizes:
	St John's Church – The Beauchamp Chapel
Worcestershire	Worcester Cathedral:
	Prince Arthur's Chapel

13

Royal Arms

The Royal Arms are shown on a shield divided into quarters (known as quartering), each quarter bearing a device.

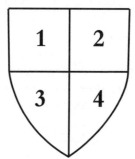

Shield showing quartering.

From the year 1405 in the reign of Henry IV, right through the Tudor Period and up to the accession of James I the Arms bore the same devices, namely:

France   – Three fleurs–de–lis, Or (gold) in first and fourth quarters on azure (blue) background.

England   – Three lions, passant guardant in pale Or on Gules (red) background in second and third quarters.

Royal Arms,
Henry IV to James I.

During the second half of the fifteenth century coats of arms were augmented by artists and seal engravers by placing two creatures, one on either side of the shield. At first these seem to have been chosen by whim and were not regarded as an integral part of the coat of arms. As they increased in popularity and as they actually supported the shield, the heralds began to take an interest and to devise rules for their control and inheritance.

Although they were, at first, not taken very seriously it was the Tudor heralds who began to rationalise their use and to bring them within the boundaries of strict armorial practice.

The Royal Arms are normally painted on wood, canvas or plaster, carved in stone or wood, moulded in plaster or cast in metal. The early examples were usually painted direct on to a panel, made up of several boards and framed. They may be found in many parts of the church, for example, over the chancel arch or screen, on north or south nave wall, usually near the west end over the north or south door and over the tower arch.

Initially, the churchwardens would approach a sign-painter or if the Arms were to be in wood, plaster, stone or cast metal another craftsman. The sign-painter would, most likely, have been an itinerant painter or a resident in a nearby town who would be employed to produce the Commandment Boards, Lord's Prayer, Creeds, hatchments and other mural paintings such as 'Sentences' which adorned Stuart and Georgian churches.

Henry VIII (1509–1547)

Royal Arms were introduced into our churches after the breach with Rome in 1534 although they are not directly coupled with the Reformation. There is no known order of Henry VIII as to his Arms being placed in places of worship.

These Arms are quite separate from the display of Royal Arms preceding this date such as those of Edward IV found, carved in stone, over the north porch of Thaxted church, Essex, and who gave the porch. Other examples may be found in stained glass as in York Minster where the nave clerestory, south side, displays the Arms of King Edward I (1272 – 1307).

Although one might assume that Arms would be hung at and following the time when Henry VIII established himself as 'Supreme Head on Earth of the church in England' there does not appear to be an order to this effect. It would appear that there is only one example of the Royal Arms of Henry VIII which is at Rushbrooke, Suffolk, but there can be no doubt that the placing of Royal Arms in our churches during this reign must have been a fairly frequent occurrence. The churchwardens' accounts at Yatton church, Avon, for 1541–2, record a payment, 'To a gylter of Bristow for gylting ye King's armys' and again at Bletchingley, Surrey, there was paid in 1546 £6 15s 2d 'for painting the quire and the rood loft, the King's Arms'. In the churchwardens' accounts of Long Melford and Wangford, Suffolk, payments were made for painting the King's Arms.

Edward VI (1547–1553)

A number of Essex churches also record the painting and hanging of the Royal Arms. At Wix, Essex, the Inventory of 1552 mentions, 'a cloth stayned and wrytte with the scripture, the Kings Majestys Arms in the middle, which cloth is hanging upon the candell-beam' (rood loft).

Again at Pagglesham £2 3s 4d was paid for, 'paynting the King's Arms and wrytting of the scriptures within the church'. And at St Mary's, Maldon, 6s 8d was paid, 'for one hundred of gold for the King's Majesties Arms and 12d for one pottall of oyle for the same'.

The systematic destruction of roods and images was an integral part of the Reformation programme in the sixteenth century. There does not appear to be any trace of an authority for the pulling down of Roods but it is likely that either there was some order made or the destruction was carried out under the Injunctions of 1547, Edward VI. These Injunctions were for a general visitation of the whole country and included instructions for the Visitors, 'That the Visitors were required to take down images before which candles were burnt including pictures and stained glass windows'. It is said that 'they pulled down all indifferently'. There is no doubt, however, that at the close of Edward's reign a large number of Roods had been destroyed and an equally large number of Royal Arms, replacing the Arms of his father, Henry VIII, had been put up in their place.

Mary (1553–1558)

The accession of Henry's Catholic daughter Mary saw great effort during her short reign to reverse all that had taken place since 1534, including the removal of the Royal Arms from their position over the Rood screen or altar, although there were no definite orders to destroy them. Bishop Gilbert in his *History of the Reformation of the Church of England* (1679), says that, 'Cardinal Pole caused Dr. Storey to visit every parish to see the Rood Lofts supplied, the crucifixes to be placed with the images of our Blessed Lady and St John, the one on the right hand and the other on the left and the King's Arms to be removed from the altar and *to be set in a place more convenient*'. It would seem, therefore, that the attempt of reversal accounts for the destruction (which is no doubt meant by the words 'to be set in a place more convenient') of Royal Arms of the previous two reigns and that none was put up in Mary's reign.

The reversal of policy, however, has left us with one example of the Arms of Henry VIII at Rushbrooke, Suffolk, and one of Edward VI at Westerham,

Kent. With regard to the Rushbrooke Royal Arms doubt has been expressed by D. MacCullock writing in the *Proceedings of the Suffolk Institute of Archaeology* XXXII (1972) 193–7, 279, and referred to in H. Munro-Cautley's book, *Suffolk Churches* (1975). The article notes that in 1840 the Royal Arms do not appear to have been in the church, while in 1855 they were said to be of modern introduction. Although apparently earlier than Victorian, they are 'suspiciously like the work of Col. Rushbrooke, that amateur Victorian craftsman to whom the church owes its present appearance'. Mr Munro Cautley, however, in his book, *Royal Arms* (1934) states that the evidence that the Rushbrooke Arms are those of Henry VIII is unusually strong. He goes on to say that they are Tudor and have the stamp of early work, the supporters being a dragon on the dexter and a greyhound on the sinister which is evidence of this period. Henry VII greatly favoured the red dragon (claiming descent from Cadwalader, last native ruler of Britain, to whom the dragon was attributed) and used it on the dexter in conjunction with a greyhound as the sinister supporter. The greyhound was a popular badge of the Lancastrian kings and special importance was placed on this royal beast by Henry VII as it symbolised, and maybe made more substantial, his tenuous links with the House of Lancaster.

Henry VIII, however, did not use just two supporters but rang the changes using the dragon and greyhound in the early Arms and the crowned lion (dexter) and red dragon (sinister) in later Arms.

Elizabeth I (1558–1603)

After the horrors associated with religion in Mary's reign, although not entirely limited to those years, there was a rapid and well-supported return to the principle of the Reformation. the Penal laws of the period against those who failed to conform to the established religion were so severe as to automatically exclude such persons from public life.

Real growth was slow, for on Queen Elizabeth's accession, although the priesthood may have consented to the changes of ritual and doctrine imposed upon them they were inwardly utterly hostile to the spirit of Protestantism and though forced to read the homilies from the pulpit the spirit of their teaching remained unchanged. It is recorded that if proclamations ordered to be read in church were not to the liking of the clergy, they were evaded by reading them to empty benches after the congregation had left the church. Later, however, when the older generation had passed away, the younger clergy filled with the spirit of Protestantism made full use of the now freed pulpit to impress, in their own manner, the religious ideas of the new generation on their congregations and so the country slowly but surely became Protestant.

Since 1689 the idea, held in England, that religion and politics can be separated would have seemed dangerous to Tudor men and women of whatever religious denomination. William Camden (1551–1623), historian, in his book, *Annales* (1615), says that, 'there can be no separation between religion and the commonwealth'. Both Henry VIII and Elizabeth aimed for a State Church that would embrace all their subjects and provide a link between the sovereign and the Church. This greater religious freedom, as well as increasing prosperity, brought about intense feelings of loyalty to the Crown which resulted in the Royal Arms being put up in churches many of which had phrases such as 'God Save the Queen'. The supporters used were the lion (dexter) and dragon (sinister).

Some examples to be seen are:

Preston, Suffolk	Tryptych. Opens to six feet four inches wide by three feet ten inches high. 'Elizabertha magna Regina Angliae'. Believed to be of Edward IV but repainted in Elizabeth's reign.
Kenninghall, Norfolk	A large crudely painted board now fixed in the tower arch but which at one time formed the tympanum over the rood screen. Inscribed, 'God save the Queen. E.R.'
Ludham, Norfolk	The tympanum of the chancel arch is entirely filled up with boarding. On the east side are the Royal Arms and on the west side an old painting of the Rood. The Arms are very faded but the inscription may still be read: 'Non me pudet Evangelium Christi (I am not ashamed of the Gospel of Christ) Vivat Regina Elizabethe'.
Waltham Abbey, Essex	Carved in wood. Portions of carved frame are missing. Arms and supporters are complete but Royal motto is missing.
Portchester, Hampshire	Dated 1577. Remarkable because the panel is lozenge shaped which is usually associated with hatchments.
Beckington, Wiltshire	Believed to be the only example carved in stone. It is built into the wall and is inscribed, 'E.R. Anno 1547 God Save the Queen'.
Greens Norton, Northamptonshire	Painted on wood with a pediment flanked by two small wooden acorns. Inscribed 'E.R.' and

	dated 1592. Faded label bearing the words 'God Save the Queen'.
Lower Quinton, Gloucestershire	The Arms cover the whole of the wall above the chancel arch where there was formerly a painted doom, traces of which are still apparent. The Arms are badly faded but the inscription is clear – 'God save our noble Queen Elizabeth. Amen'.
Sandford, St Martin, Oxfordshire	Over the chancel arch facing the altar. Painted on wooden boards and filling most of the triangular space. Dated 1602 and bearing what are believed to be the names of the churchwardens of 1601 – 'John Studdey, Richard Appletree. Churchmen'. It is believed possible that these Arms were moved to this position at the time of the restorations of 1856. Probably, in the re-fixing, part of the bottom was mutilated as the feet on which the lion and dragon stand are missing together with any inscription there may have been.
Elton, Hereford & Worcester	A fine piece of carving in oak in bold relief but no colour. It is surrounded by a carved frame. Initialled 'E.R.' and inscribed, 'God save the Queene'.

James I (1603–1625)

Royal Arms, James I to James II (excluding Commonwealth 1649–1660).

When James VI of Scotland succeeded to the throne of England as James I in 1603 there occurred four changes to the Royal Arms of England. The Dragon which had supported the sinister side of the Arms of Elizabeth I was replaced by the Unicorn which had been the badge of the Stuarts since the reign of James III (1460–1488). The other changes were to the marshalling of the shield.

The former Royal Arms of England were quartered within the first and fourth quarters. Into the second quarter went the Arms of the King of Scots and in the third quarter the opportunity was then taken to incorporate the Arms of Ireland representing the hereditary title King of Ireland which had been granted to Henry VIII in 1541 by an Act of the Irish parliament. This new Royal Arms thus represented all that the royal style proclaimed: the Kingdom of Great Britain – England and Scotland – and the Kingdoms of Ireland and France supported by the Lion of England and the Unicorn of Scotland. These Arms are correctly referred to in England as the Stuart Arms.

It seems that a very large number of churches possessed the Royal Arms of James and this, corroborated by a licence granted by Archbishop Abbot in 1614 to John Serjent, a painter-stainer of Hitchin, in which it is stated that 'Royal Arms are set up in all or most part of the Churches and Chappells within the said realm', but instructing him 'to survey and paynt in all the churches and chappells within the Realm of England, the Kinges Majesties Armes in due form, with helme, crest, mantell, and supporters as they ought to be, together with the noble young prince's [Charles I b. 1600], and to wrighte in fayre text letters, the tenn commandments, the beliefs and the Lord's prayer, with some other fruitful and profitable sentences of holye scryptue'.

It is impossible, without initials or dates, as with the Tudors, to identify any of the Stuart Arms except in the case of William and Mary and that part of Anne's reign after 1707. There are, however, two ways to enable positive identification to be made (1) if the initial letters are floriated. This is so sure a guide that if one sees any Arms initialled 'G.R.' even if the shield is charged for Hanover and the letters are floriated, one may be sure that they were formerly Stuart Arms brought up to date in the Hanoverian period; and (2) when one sees the motto, 'Exurgat Deus Dissinentur Inimici' (Let God arise and let His enemies be scattered) which would have been very applicable in the case of James I. Examples with this inscription may be seen on Arms at Blisland, Cornwall, painted on wood and dated 1604 on the ornamental border. Troston, Suffolk, where the initials 'G.R.' have been added, probably by an economically minded Hanoverian churchwarden. Hilborough, Norfolk, has initials 'I.R.' with a date which is probably 1611 but is rather clumsily painted on boards with the date at the bottom between representations of roses and thistles of rather large proportions. Mention must be made of two magnificent examples of this reign (1) at Winsford, Somerset, initialled 'I.R.' and dated 1609, painted on wood. It is about seven feet square and is inscribed with a text from Ecclesiastes 10:20; and (2) perhaps the most imposing, at Wisbech,

Cambridgeshire, which is carved out of wood about eight inches thick and about eight feet square. Records are still extant, dated 27th May 1605 recording that. 'It was agreed that Robert Buckstone should be forthwith paid fower pounds for the furnishing the King's Majesties Arms in the Parish Church of Wisbeche'.

Charles I (1625–1649)

There are few instances in which the Arms of Charles I remain in our churches as they were generally pulled down and destroyed during the Commonwealth. Parliament, at this time, was beginning to be aware that it had duties beyond those of supplying financial aid and moral support for royal disposition; it was imbued with self-determination and with a king, who was, perhaps, 'High Church, but was not a Catholic' it is difficult to see why the Church should have been so insistent in putting up Royal Arms in our churches. Perhaps it was urged to do so by fear of the power and influence willed by Charles' Catholic consort, Henrietta Marie. Whatever the reason a licence was issued by Archbishop Abbott early in the reign to Thomas Hanbage, paynter-stayner. Following the preliminaries the licence goes on to say,

> And whereas there ought to be had an especiall care that all churches and chapells within this Kingdome of England be beautified and adorned with Godly sentences and more especially with his Majesties Armes and the Tenne Commandments, yett in some place the same is altogether neglected, and in other places suffered to be defaced. We, therefore, as much as is in us, duly weighing the premisses, and having a care for the redresse thereof, doe hereby give you the sayd Thomas Hanbage, leave, licence and authority to go and take a review of the ruines of the parish churches within my diocese of Canterbury, and in and through all the peculiar jurisdictions of us and of our cathedrall, and after a review so had to show yourself ready and willing to paynte his Majesties Arms with the Tenne Commandments and other holy sentences upon some eminent places within the Chauncells or Bodyes of the sayd churches, where now they are wantinge, and where those Armes be defaced, in colours or otherwise, that for the better adornage of the said churches the same be beautified with helmett Crest and mantle, as in most churches of England the same are now adorned you takinge for your paynes an honest and reasonable allowance, wishing thereby all Persons, Vicars, Curats, Churchwardens, Sidesmen and all other officers of the severall churches aforesaid, that they to their best powers give you admittance as is fit in the performance of the premises ... Dated 24th. October 1631.

As in the case of all periods prior to the Commonwealth, and for obvious reasons, Royal Arms were not popular and must have been destroyed in vast numbers so that there are few examples left to see.

Suffolk, however, has five examples:

1. Knettishall (now disused), had a fine set of Charles I Arms dated 1632. In 1666 in the reign of Charles II following the Restoration, the last two figures were transparently painted over with two sixes. These Arms are now in Riddlesworth church, Norfolk.

2. Mellis church has Arms dated 1634 which hang at the west end.

3. At Ashbocking church the Arms are dated 1640 and inscribed 'God Save the King'. They still hang on the south wall where they were defiantly maintained by Theodore Beadle the Royalist vicar who ultimately died in the hulks on the River Thames as a prisoner of Parliament. The registers of this period of this loyal parish are ended by the signatures of the churchwardens and 'God Save the King'.

4. Denham church has Arms dated 1637 which hang high above the chancel arch.

5. The Arms at Ampton church are of great interest. They are cut out of wood approximately one inch thick similar to fretwork. The design, although in fairly good condition has, unfortunately, suffered damage to the letter 'C' and part of the lion is not very distinct. The reason for the condition of the painting is said to be because the colouring medium used was distemper which has mostly gone. There was a date which is believed to have been 1636 but the distemper was so loose on the wood that it has disappeared. Restoration work has been taken to preserve the colouring which is still left. The Arms are approximately four feet six inches square and in all probability stood on a former screen as the tenons remain at the bottom and as was usual with Arms set on a screen was coloured on both sides. On each side of the Arms is a coloured and crowned badge, the one on the dexter representing the Thistle of Scotland and on the sinister the Rose of England fixed to iron spikes.

At Furneaux Pelham, Hertfordshire, there is a small set of Arms on top of a screen, one side dated 1634 and the other 1660.

Abbey Dore, Hereford & Worcester, has a fine set of Arms on top of a most interesting chancel screen in the magnificent remains of this great Cistercian Abbey, the transepts and choir of which now form the parish church.

In Essex, at Messing, there is a very interesting set dated 1634. The board hangs free in the south transept. It is carved and painted wood on a pedimented wooden backing with the initials 'C.R.' and is dated 1634. The backing is formed of two panels, the Arms being on the upper one and on the lower one is the following inscription: 'Timothy 3:1–2; 2 Timothy 2:22–4; 1Thess 5:21; Luke 2:14; Ephesians 6:24.' On the frame between the panels is another inscription, 'My sonne feare thou the Lord and the King: And meddle not with them that are given to change Prov. 24'. The reverse side of the board is also decorated. The top panel contains the Prince of Wales' Feathers, a Crown, the letters C P. and the same date 1634. The lower panel contains the achievement of Arms of Hanameel Chibborne and his wife. On the frame between the panels on this side is inscribed 'Give thy judgements to the King O Lord Thy Righteousness to the King's Sonn'.

Charles I was tried and executed in 1649 and the Monarchy and Lords were abolished. England was proclaimed a Commonwealth.

Commonwealth (1649–1660)

From 1648 to 1707 the Arms were six times superseded by variant coats which reflect in their composition the political upheavals and changes which the monarchy experienced. Firstly the Stuart Arms were abolished during the Commonwealth. From 1648 to 1655 there was 'The State Arms' which carefully avoided any recollection of royal heraldry. In 1655 new Arms were designed for the Protectorate which were very interesting as they referred to the Tudor Arms and reflected the attempts to establish a limited Parliamentary monarchy in the House of Cromwell. Over the shield which contained national emblems – England, St George (1 & 4); Scotland, St Andrew (2); Ireland, harp (3). In the centre of the shield was Oliver Cromwell's Arms 'over all' on a small shield. Over the top of the Arms was a royal helmet bearing the former royal crown and crest. The dexter supporter was the Lion and the Dragon was revived as the sinister supporter. Although not general a few State Arms were set up in churches and the churchwardens' accounts for St Leonard's, Hythe, Colchester, Essex, contains an entry in 1647, 'for setting up the State Arms 14s 6d'. If this date is correct it would appear to be an early snub at authority. In September 1660, there is a payment of 1s 'for to get out the State Arms'. (This information was obtained from *Royal Arms* by H. Munro-Cautley.) At North Walsham, Norfolk, is an unusual set of Arms of Charles II, dated 1661 on one side of the board whilst on the other side is a Commonwealth device!

Charles II (1660–1685)

Charles II in the year following his father's death came over from France and was crowned King at Scone, repudiating his father's acts and his mother's faith for the purpose. He had a substantial following in Scotland but like his grandfather, he could not profit from the mistakes of his predecessors and whereas he might have had the affection of the people he alienated that affection by his lack of principle and his flagrant debauchery. Charles invaded England in 1651 but was defeated by Cromwell at Worcester and fled, in exile, to France where he remained for nine years. In 1660 Charles returned to England on 25 May and was met with an unprecedented welcome which showed how short was the public's memory.

Following the restoration of Charles in 1660 a statute requiring that the Royal Arms should be displayed in all churches resulted in many old boards being brought out of hiding, repainted and new ones made.

Early examples were inscribed 'God save the King' as at Alpheton and Rendham, Suffolk and at St Kew, Cornwall, where the Arms are in plaster about seven feet by six feet with a triangular pediment and dated 1661. The welcome soon wore thin and later examples are without the inscription. In the parish registers of Warrington, Lancashire, there is an entry dated 30 July 1660, 'Whereas it is generally enjoined by the Great Counsell of England that in all churches thorowout the Kingdom of England his Majesties Arms shall be sett up ...'

The Royal Arms of this period are numerous and are to be found in any part of the country. Some examples are:

Ipswich, Suffolk:	St Margaret. Beautiful set of Arms in a very fine carved frame.
Laindon, Essex:	St Mary the Virgin and All Saints. The Arms are distempered on the plasterwork of the tympanum resting on a tie-beam between nave and chancel and dated 1660. Beneath the Arms is the text, 'My son feare thou the Lord and the King and meddle not with them that are given to change Prov. xxiv,21. John Elliott churchwarden of Laindon'.
Wickhamford, Hereford and Worcester:	Over the chancel arch the Arms dated 1661 reach up to the panelled roof of the celure.
Beccles, Suffolk:	In the tower is a set of Arms made of board cut and pierced. It is similarly coloured on both sides but much of the colour has disappeared. It is framed and interestingly has nails all the way round the frame which probably held the strained canvas of a later achievement of Arms.
Great Baddow, Essex:	Over the chancel arch painted on wood

surrounded with a moulded frame and surmounted with a pediment. Initialled 'C.R.' and
dated 1660. Restored in 1963.

The county of Cornwall contains a large number of Charles II Arms including fourteen plasterwork Arms which are all of a similar but not identical design. This county was formerly noted for the large number of elaborate Royal Arms the majority of which were of Restoration date. Unfortunately the large majority were destroyed during the latter part of the nineteenth century by the 'restorers'. At this stage in the chapter reference must be made to the care which should be exercised by the reader in dating Royal Arms. The initials and dates shown must be evaluated against all other evidence. For example, the Arms of Charles I at Lanteglos, Cornwall are clearly dated 1668 but it is obvious that the last two figures have later been clumsily altered to conform with the Order of Parliament in 1660. These Arms were originally painted in his father's reign. This was an act of economy on the part of the churchwardens so that a new set of Arms would not be necessary. The Arms of Charles II at Poughill, Cornwall, are dated 1655 when Cromwell was in power!

Most of the altered Arms will be of the reign of Charles II because it was only in this and subsequent reigns that the display of Arms became compulsory. In order to save the expense of a new set of Arms, churchwardens who cared nothing about heraldry would get the village painter to change the 'C' for a 'G' in the case of a George following a Charles and to alter the date.

At Vange in Essex, the Arms are painted on wood and the old initials have been painted out and 'W.R. 1689' painted in their place. This is obvious by reason of the fact that the Nassau inescutcheon was omitted and so the Arms were updated.

At Hawkedon, Suffolk, the Arms were originally those of Charles II with probably 'God Save the King' on the label but the 'C' was changed to a 'G' and the label painted out and inscribed with the Royal motto and the date 1750.

An interesting set of Arms of Charles II is in Burstwick church, Humberside. It is painted on deal boards, lozenge shaped, about fifty-four inches square and hangs under an arch of the north arcade so that the reverse may be seen. The achievement is inscribed 'ANNO DOM:1676' 'C.R.'. In an oval at the bottom of the Arms is the inscription 'God save the King'. Obviously the Arms were originally for Charles I. It is the reverse of the Arms which is remarkable as it depicts the execution of Charles I with the scaffolding set up in a crowded Whitehall with the Banqueting Hall in the background which is also crowded with onlookers, some of whom are on the roof ridge. On the scaffold the executioner holds up the decapitated head of the King. The painting is taken from a copper plate engraving published at Amsterdam in 1649. There is a long Latin inscription above the picture and in the top corner is the inscription, 'Januarie Die XXX. MDCXLVIII' and in the bottom corner, 'I.C. Huius Ecclesiae Vic'. The date is the date of the execution and the remainder is, 'John Catlyn Vicar of this church'. The painting was placed in the church by John Catlyn in 1676. He was vicar from 1670 to 1678 and was a great royalist.

James II (1685–1689)

James succeeded quietly to the throne on the death of his brother in 1685. He made no secret of the fact that he was a Roman Catholic and at the coronation service he declined to receive the communion according to the rites of the Church of England.

In various ways James took steps to restore the Catholic faith and appointed Catholic officials wherever possible. For example the privy seal was held by Lord Arundel of Wardour, the Lord High Admiral was the King himself, one of the two secretaries of state was the Earl of Middleton and two privy councillors were Nicholas Butler, a convert, and Edward Petre, a Jesuit. The ruling policy was not merely of advancing Romanist individuals but also parish institutions. It seemed likely that James might follow Mary's example and try to lead the country back to Rome. James, however, liked to pose as the champion of toleration and in 1687 and 1688 he issued Declarations of Indulgence in which he declared his protection for the established Church but, nevertheless, suspended all penal laws against nonconformists, Roman Catholics and others. Although the Archbishop of Canterbury, William Sancroft, and six other bishops petitioned the King to withdraw it he declined and the seven bishops were imprisoned in the Tower of London and brought to trial for seditious libel. A verdict of, 'Not guilty' was brought and received with great acclamation by the people. A few days before the trial the Queen bore a son and this gave further impetus to the dissenters in the country to bring the Stuart dynasty to an end.

Approaches were made to William of Orange and his wife Mary, daughter of James II by his first wife, Anne Hyde, and in July 1688 they were formally invited. There was much unrest which affected the whole country and during this period William was collecting his forces to invade England. He landed at Torbay on 5 November and on 18 December James fled from England, dropping the Great Seal into the Thames during his flight. On the same day William entered London. Parliament declared the throne vacant and then offered it to William and Mary as joint sovereigns.

Suffolk has three examples of James II's Arms: (1) Blakenham Parva dated 1685 and initialled J 2 R; (2) Oulton, where the Arms are undated but initialled

J 2 R. These Arms are said to have come from St Margaret's, Westminster and (3) Weston. These Arms are undated but initialled J 2 R.

At Golant, Cornwall, St Sampson, the Arms are painted on wood about five feet square with a semicircular pediment. Initialled J.2D.R and dated 1685.

North Cray, Kent, has a fine example in cast iron with a beaded border, initialled J.R. and dated 1687. It is beautifully designed and is hung by chains.

Over the tower arch in Rivenhall church, Essex, is a set of Arms painted on canvas and initialled J.2d.R. The Archdeacon's visitation in 1684/5 directed that the 'King's Arms to be set up'.

At Great Snoring, Norfolk, is a very fine set of Arms with label and dated 1688. It would seem, however, that the date and label were painted on an earlier achievement.

William and Mary (1689–1702)

Royal Arms, William and Mary to Anne 1707.

William, Prince of Nassau, was the son of William II of Orange and Mary daughter of Charles I, and had been made Stadtholder (Chief Magistrate) of the United Netherlands. To represent this important position he placed the Arms of Nassau, a blue shield spattered with vertical gold rectangles and a gold lion over all, on an inescutcheon on the fess point of the Royal Arms.

Both were staunch Protestants and Mary, the daughter of James II, was probably the most honest and discreet of any of the Stuarts and having a real sense of the duties of her position. William was astute and possessed considerable character but was more concerned with Holland than England. The Church felt that now there was harmony and sympathy with it in the policy and practice of the Crown, and this may account for the number of Royal Arms of this period. Mary died in 1694.

It is well to mention that in the beginning of the reign there were variations in the Arms due to Scotland not recognising William and Mary as the sovereign in Scotland until April 1689. In fact there joint sovereignty was not established in England until February 1689 and the first version of their Arms discreetly omitted Scotland. The Arms were composed of the Arms of England in the first and fourth quarters (as in the Stuart Arms) and Ireland in the second and third quarters with the Nassau Arms superimposed on an escutcheon of pretence. The Dragon replaced the Unicorn as a Supporter. From 11 April 1689 a second version was briefly introduced when the Scots recognised the joint monarchy. This version showed a quartered shield on which England occupied the first quarter alone, Scotland the second, Ireland the third and France (modern) the fourth quarter (three fleurs-de-lis). The Arms of Nassau were superimposed on an inescutcheon of pretence. The Unicorn was readopted as a supporter. This version was short-lived and was followed by the standard form as already shown.

Some examples are:

Wyverstone, Suffolk, where there is a very fine set carved in wood.

Barnham, Suffolk, composed of painted panels. Neither of the two Suffolk examples is dated.

Gimingham, Norfolk, has a small carved set which, instead of the complete Nassau shield has a small rampant lion coloured red at the fess point. The Arms are contained in a carved frame.

Sible Hedingham, Essex, has a set carved in wood and coloured. In lieu of the royal motto it has 'je main tain dray' from the French phrase 'je maintiendrai le droit' (I will maintain the right).

Witham, Essex, has a similar set to Sible Hedingham but is coloured on both sides and was obviously designed to be placed on top of a screen. The motto is slightly different, 'je main tien dray'.

Anne (1702–1714)

Anne, the second daughter of James II was the last of the Stuarts. She had little personal accomplishment but her twelve years of rule were comparatively peaceful compared with the upheavals of earlier years. In 1704 Anne greatly pleased the Church by restoring to it the 'first fruits', annates and tenths, which had previously been confiscated by Henry VIII. The annates were the first year's revenues from an ecclesiastical benefice which had formerly been paid to the Pope. The tenths was a tenth part of the annual profit of every living paid to the Pope. In 1704 a fund was established by Queen Anne to receive the revenues from these two taxes and which was to be known as 'Queen Anne's

Bounty'. This fund was generally used to supplement the incomes of the poorer clergy.

It was merged with the Ecclesiastical Commission and formed the Church Commission for England in 1945. Perhaps it was gratitude on the part of the Church which has plentifully supplied our churches with her Arms.

Up to 1707 Anne's Arms remained unchanged from those which had prevailed throughout the Stuart period, but in that year the union with Scotland took place and the Arms of Nassau were removed. The kingdom known as Great Britain had been born and the Royal Arms were altered. By an Order in Council of April 1707 the quarters for England and France were formally separated and the Arms of England and Scotland were impaled (like the Arms of a married couple) in the first and fourth quarters. France was given the whole of the second quarter and Ireland the entire third quarter.

Royal Arms, Anne from 1707 to George I.

The floriated initial letter which characterised the Arms of the Stuart period gradually passed during Anne's reign and although many examples retain its use there are also some with plain letters as at the Black Chapel, North End, Essex, where the Arms are painted on canvas and dated 1714 with the motto, 'Semper Eadem' (Always the same). This motto is the distinguishing feature of the Arms of this period so much so that where the Arms of Charles II, at Cley, Norfolk, were adapted for Anne the motto 'Semper Eadem' was painted over the Royal motto.

Some examples to be seen are:

Hadleigh, Essex	Floriated initial letter.
Thaxted, Essex	Arms printed on wooden boards cut to the shape of the design, without initials or date. Approximately nine feet square with old Stuart Arms with motto, 'Semper Eadem'. A fine set which must be of Anne's reign prior to 1707.

Roydon, Suffolk	Dated 1713.
Lockington, Leicestershire	The tympanum above the screen is painted with the Lord's Prayer and Creed above which is the Royal Arms filling the whole width of the nave and rising to the roof. It is dated 1704 and bears the crowned initials 'A.R.'. The shield bears the old Stuart Arms. The whole is in plaster.
Portchester, Hampshire	These very fine Arms hang on the north wall with those of Elizabeth I on the south. An imposing board twelve feet long by six feet six inches high, inscribed 'By the Bounty of Queen Anne. This Church is repaired and beautified 1710'.
Redenhall, Norfolk	A large set of Arms in a gilded frame high up over the chancel arch.
Harberton, Devon	A fine set of Arms on carved and painted wood on a shaped backing board curving to a point at the top. The Arms are of 1707–1714 with the motto 'Semper'. Inscription below the Arms reads, 'Fear God, Honour the King, 1 Peter II Chap. 17 Verse' together with 'Restored by Major Trist of Tristford, A.D. 1883'.

George I (1714–1727, George II (1727–1760) and George III (1760–1811, Regency (1811–1820), George IV (1820–1830) and William IV (1830–1837)

Royal Arms, George I to George III (1801).

On Queen Anne's death in 1714 George Lewis, Elector of Hanover, became king necessitating alterations in the Royal Arms. The Act of Settlement, 1701, had decreed that if Queen Anne died without children surviving her the Crown should pass to the electress Sophia of Hanover or her heirs in order to preserve the Protestant Succession. Although Anne had innumerable children none survived her and she was succeeded by Elector George of Hanover who had become heir to the throne on the death of Princess Sophia. The Arms of George I are as for Anne with the exception of the fourth quarter which contains the Arms of the new king. The quarter was arranged as shown below:

Royal Arms, Fourth quarter.

Top left the Arms of Brunswick, two golden lions 'passant guardant' on a red background; top right for Luneberg, a blue lion 'rampant' surrounded by a number of red hearts on a gold background; below the arms of Westphalia, a silver (sometimes white) horse galloping on a red background. In the middle of the shield a smaller shield (an escutcheon of pretence) containing the Arms of office for the Arch-Treasurer of the Holy Roman Empire, a post held by the electors – the golden Crown of Charlemagne on a red background. These Arms remained until 1801 in the reign of George III.

For a period of ninety-four years, i.e. from 1707 (following the Act of Union) until 1801 there was no definite way of distinguishing these Arms except by entries in churchwardens' accounts or dates or initials on the Arms and these cannot always be relied upon. Examples exist where the Arms of Hanover have been painted over the fourth quarter and many of the date of George I have subsequently had one or two numerals added to adapt them for subsequent Georges.

Between the years 1801–1816 (George III) it became a little easier to identify the Arms as the king decided to abandon his title as King of France, so the fleurs-de-lis were removed from the English Arms. England now appears in the first and fourth quarters, Scotland in the second quarter and Ireland in the third quarter. At the centre, the 'fess point', appears the Hanoverian Arms on an escutcheon with the electoral Bonnet over, the Cap of Estate, of red velvet with an ermine brim and topped with a gold tassel as overleaf.

Royal Arms, George III
1801–1816.

One further change took place in 1816. Napoleon abolished the Holy Roman Empire in 1806 but the Arms of its office of Arch-Treasurer remained on the Hanoverian Arms and they stayed there until 1816 when the Electorate of Hanover was elevated to the dignity of a kingdom at the Congress of Vienna and the bonnet was changed by an Order in Council, 8 June 1816, to a royal crown.

These Arms remained unaltered during the remainder of the reign of George III who died in 1820. George suffered from senile porphyria and it became necessary for Parliament to pass the Regency Act on 5 February 1811 whereby his son, George, Prince of Wales, was appointed Regent (1811–1820). On the death of George III his son, George became king. George IV died on 4 June 1830 and was succeeded by his brother Duke of Clarence as William IV. On 20 June 1837 William died and was succeeded by his niece Victoria.

Royal Arms, George III,
(1816–Victoria).

Examples of Arms of George I, II, III and IV and William IV to be seen are:

George I

Long Melford, Suffolk   A fine set carved in wood over south door.

Lymington, Hampshire   Large panel in west porch. It was originally painted with the Arms of Charles II but was re-painted in 1716 for George I by John Cleeves. The initial 'C' was altered to 'G', the escutcheon of the House of Hanover was inserted and the original date over the Arms was altered from MDCLXXVI to MDCCXVI. The names of the later churchwardens, William Chappell and William Scorell were substituted for the original names of Robert Edwards and John Huxton and the date 1716 are at the bottom of the Arms.

Little Clacton, Essex	The Arms above the north door are painted on board about four feet square, initialled 'G.R.' and dated 1726.
Abbotsbury, Dorset	A fine set in front of gallery.
Stoke Rivers, Devon	On west wall of south aisle. Painted on wood in a white frame with rounded top five feet by six feet six inches. Initialled 'G.R.' A fine set restored in the early 1970s.
St Erth, Cornwall	On the north wall. Arms painted on wood and initialled 'G.R.' A fine set restored by Elizabeth Cynddylan in 1979.
Hatfield Broad Oak, Essex	Over chancel arch. Painted on wood or canvas with a semicircular top and contained in an ornate golden frame. Initialled 'G.R.'

George II

Mildenhall, Suffolk	A large set of Arms dated 1758.
Cranbrook, Kent	A beautifully carved set inscribed 'These Arms were the gift of Thomas Basden Apothecary in London in the year 1756.'
Landulph, Cornwall	Over south door. Painted on wood with an ornamented top in a decorated black and white frame about four feet square. Initialled 'G.II.R.' Restored *c.*1976.
Fobbing, Essex	A fine set over south door. Painted and carved wood on a blue backing cut roughly to shape of carving. The unicorn has a real chain.

Sulhamstead, Abbots, Berkshire	On the east wall of the nave. Painted on canvas, approximately five feet square. Dated 1750 and initialled 'G.R.'

George III

Brampton, Suffolk	A set inscribed 'God save the King 1 Samuel X chap. 24 ver' dated 1797.
Dolton, Devon	Over south door. Painted on wood about five feet square. Dated 1760 and initialled 'G III R.'
Southwold, Suffolk	North aisle. Set initialled 'G.R.III' and dated 1783 in gilt frame. Very good condition.
Salle, Norfolk	Dated 1790. Good condition.

1801 – 1816

Harlaxton, Lincolnshire	On nave north wall this set is painted on a canvas quatrefoil. On lower lobe is inscribed, 'G. de Ligne Gregory Esq. Rev. H. Dodwell Rector. Rev. Thos. Haskett & T. Harvey Chwardens'. The whole Arms are enclosed by a red and ermine cloak with a second crest of the Prince of Wales' feathers above set against a skyscape background.
Belstone, Devon	West wall of north aisle. Painted on wood about four feet six inches square. Initialled 'G.III R'.
Sancreed, Cornwall	On south wall of nave at west end. Painted on wood about four feet by three feet six inches. Arms of 1714–1801 initialled 'GIIIR'.
Little Coxwell, Berkshire	On chancel arch. Painted on canvas about five feet square.
Black Notley, Essex	Over south door. Painted on canvas six feet square. Dated 1802.

George IV

Burnham Norton, Norfolk	The Arms are inscribed 'Zech Fenn 1826 Painter Walsingham'.
Edenham, Lincolnshire	Above the chancel arch. This set is carved in artificial stone (Coade stone) on a rectangular

	block about six feet by four feet and painted. Signed 'Coade:London:1820' Errors in colours.
South Kelsey, Lincolnshire	High over tower arch. Appears to be painted on canvas about two feet six inches square. Initialled 'G.R.IV' across the top.
Easton-on-the-Hill, Northamptonshire	Arms dated 1826 and signed 'T. Simpson Penxt Stamford'.
Barnby, Suffolk	Arms dated 1825 and signed 'Hall Penxt'. A fine set.
Creed, Cornwall	North wall of nave. A fine set painted on wood with semicircular pediment in a pink marbled frame about seven feet by six feet. Initialled 'G.IV.R.' Signed at bottom 'T. Barlow. Painter Truro'.

William IV

Knutsford, Cheshire	Arms dated 1831. Inscription on accompanying board reads 'These Arms were painted in the 2nd. of the reign of his most gracious Majesty KING WILLIAM the fourth, by Robt. Haward AE;72'.
Countisbury, Devon	On west wall. Painted on wood about three feet by four feet. Dated, in corners of frame, 1–8–3–7 and inscribed at the top, 'GULIELMUS IV – BRITT. REX.'
Cuby, Cornwall	Over south door. Painted on wood about two feet six inches by four feet. Initialled 'W.R.' and dated 1831. The Hanoverian white horse is on a black field and Charlemagne is white. The set is rather crude but has been restored by Elizabeth Cynddylan in 1978.
West Mersea, Essex	Over north door. Carved and painted wood. Dated 1823. The supporters are emerging from behind the shield. The Arms are in a fair condition.

Victoria (1830–1901)

Women were unable to succeed to the Hanoverian throne (the Salic Law) so

Royal Arms, Victoria to
Elizabeth II.

this country's continental links were severed and the Victorian Arms are as
before but with the central Hanoverian shield removed and so they have
remained unchanged.

The Arms of the period 1830 to 1901 decline steadily in quality and become
fewer in number until about the middle of the nineteenth century when they
practically cease.

Examples of Victoria's Arms can be seen at:

Evesham, Hereford & Worcester	Painted probably on canvas and framed.
Aldbury, Hertfordshire	Painted on wood and framed with semicircular pediment. Initialled 'V.R.' and dated 1838.
Bury St Edmunds, (St Mary) Suffolk	Top of screen. Possibly cast iron or plaster. Well coloured.
Tonge, Kent	An interesting set modelled in iron about twenty-two and a half inches in height and width. Made by Coalbrookdale Company Ironworks. It would seem to be made in pieces which are bolted together at the back. No trace of painting.
Elmdon, Essex	Over door east end of south aisle. Cast in iron, probably from the Coalbrookdale Company, and brightly coloured. The Arms came from St Dunstan's, Wenden Lofts, Essex.
Washbrook, Suffolk	A fine set in plaster.

Examples of modern Arms following from Queen Victoria:

Edward VII (1901–1910)

Oxford, St Michael, Northgate	West window. Painted glass. Royal shield initialled 'E VII'.
Onibury, Shropshire	West gallery. Carved and painted wood. Initialled 'ED VII' in carved letters at top.

George V (1910–1936)

(Very rare)

Hampton Gay, Oxfordshire	On gallery at west end. Carved wood and painted, one foot square. Within a frame which is rather wide for size of Arms. Initialled 'G.V.' and 'R'. On a strip fixed to frame is 'Carved by Alfred A. Miller'.
Englishcombe, Somerset	Painted in 1917.
Ickford, Buckinghamshire	Believed to be dated 1913.
Trentishoe, Devon	On west gallery. Colour transfers on a polished wood backing, lozenge-shaped. Dated 1911 and initialled 'G.R.'

Edward VIII (1936)

None known to author.

George VI (1936–1952)

None known to author.

Elizabeth II (1952–)

Bodicote, Oxfordshire	Initialled 'E.R.' In full colour.
Cotleigh, Devon	Over door to west tower. Painted on wood. Dated 1977 for Silver Jubilee.
Upjohn, Devon	On north gallery. Arms carved in wood and painted. About two feet six inches by three feet. For Coronation.
Little Baddow, Essex	Painted on wood with black background. Initialled 'E-II R'.
Great Braxted, Essex	Over vestry door. Painted on wood.

14

Church Chests

Large chests or coffers, having the front formed of a single panel, were in common domestic and civil use throughout the Middle Ages and so they naturally found their way into churches where they were used for the safe keeping of vestments, ornaments, plate, documents and other valuables. Probably every church and almost every chantry or guild had its chest, 'ark', 'coffer' or 'hutch' and some churches possessed several chests.

The earliest chests to be found are pre-Conquest but they are rare. They continued until the Georgian period after which they again became rare being superseded by chests of drawers for domestic use but were of little use in churches.

During some eight hundred years there was considerable development in the art and skill required which allows the various types to be classified. This

GREAT BURSTEAD, ESSEX.
Dug-out chest C12–13.

is shown by the ingenious hinge construction of the lids and the iron banding and locks as well as the construction of chests, for example, boarded, stiled and coved. The work was not often carried out by skilled craftsmen, most of it being the work of the local carpenter and blacksmith.

Oak was the primary timber used but it is possible to come across chests made of elm, chestnut, sycamore, cedar or cypress.

The oldest and simplest form of large chest or coffer to be found in parish churches is a dug-out chest simply constructed out of a hugh baulk of oak or other tree. A slice was cut from the trunk and the remaining portion was roughly squared externally with an axe and a cavity gouged out of the top, a difficult and laborious job. The portion which was first cut away was replaced as a lid over the hole and fitted with hinges and locks of iron.

As may be imagined the gouging out of a cavity in a baulk of oak was extremely laborious especially with the tools of the time which were primitive compared with modern standards. A type of axe known as an adze was more commonly used for this purpose. Because of this difficulty the cavity was small and in the case of the Wimborne Minster chest, which is six and a half feet long, the cavity is only twenty-two inches long, nine inches wide and six inches deep. This chest is believed to have been used for keeping relics safe and no doubt they were, for with no joints to prise apart, thieves would have had to try to split open the log. The lid was very thick and in the middle ages six great iron locks were fitted, parts of which still remain. It is believed that this was the strong box of the Saxon nunnery in which relics, documents and other treasures were preserved some eleven hundred years ago. In the eighteenth century a number of documents in the chest were examined and some were found to date back to 1200.

Some dug-out chests have larger cavities but these have probably had the original cavity enlarged at a later date. The Injunctions of Archbishop Aelfric (995–1005) gave evidence that chests were included in the furniture of a Saxon church and that they were needed not because they were ordered.

The first definite order was given in the year 1166 when the mandate of Henry II ordered that boxes or chests be placed in parish churches in England wherein the faithful were expected to deposit money for the prosecution of the Crusades. The money collected in these boxes or chests was to be sent annually to the knights of the great Military Orders in Palestine for the Crusades. The chests were to be secured with three locks, the keys to which were to be held, one in the custody of the priest and the other two by two trustworthy parishioners.

The money so collected was to be sent to the Templars and Hospitallers to accumulate until the time that Henry arrived to lead the armies. Although he twice took the vows and the cross of a crusader he never kept his promises and the accumulated wealth stored in the treasury of the House of the Hospitallers was finally put into the common fund for the redemption of the Christian captives after Jerusalem was taken by Saladin in 1187.

A similar Order to that of Henry II was issued by Pope Innocent III on 31 December 1199. It was sent to the archbishops and bishops of Tuscany, Lombardy, Germany, France, England, Hungary, Slavonia, Ireland and Scotland, for them to raise funds for the fifth crusade. To this end he commanded that in every church there should be placed a hollow trunk, fastened with three keys, the first to be kept by the bishop, the second by the priest of the church and the third by some religious layman; that the faithful should be exhorted to deposit in it, according as God moved their hearts, their alms for the remission of their sins and that once in the week, in all churches, mass should be publicly sung for the remission of sins and especially of those who should thus contribute. The money deposited in the church chests was called 'Saladin's Tithe' and was collected and amassed in Salisbury – a total of £6,000, a large sum in those days.

An additional safety precaution was to bind the dug-out chest with numerous iron bands. This precaution persisted long after dug-outs and some of the iron work was very decorative. Some chests, like the one at Hatfield, South Yorkshire, were studded with iron nails as well as being bound with iron.

It is difficult to determine the date of these chests but most authorities are convinced that the majority of dug-outs are of Norman, twelfth century, date, although there are a few of pre-Norman date, e.g. the Saxon chest at Wimborne Minster, Dorset. They were also occasionally made for a time after the Norman period. Many of these chests must be ascribed to the Royal Order of 1166 whilst others were to satisfy the demands of Pope Innocent III.

The working of timber and the fashioning of ironwork and locks very much depended upon the skill of the local joiner and smith which meant that whilst beautiful scroll work was produced in a period in one district, rough and sometimes primitive results would be obtained during the same period in another district.

The earliest example of a dug-out chest in Essex is probably the one in Langham church. It contains a very small cavity, one foot one inch long, seven inches wide and six inches deep whilst the whole chest is four feet seven inches long, one foot six inches wide and one foot three inches deep. It is made of coarse-grained oak, rugged in appearance and has, obviously, received rough usage. The lid is bound with iron across the ends of the grain and has two hinges across it and extending some distance over the top of the chest to which they are fixed with nails and two staples to each. Across the middle of the lid extends another iron strap which originally carried the hasp of the lock. The five iron bands, almost covering the surface of the lid, are thickly studded with nails. In the middle band of iron is a money slot which presupposes that this was originally designed as a money chest and probably the result of the Order of Henry II, 1166, in which money was collected for his projected conquest of Jerusalem but which never materialised. This probably explains the broken hasp and recess in the front of the chest where there was originally the lock and its large plate which has obviously been forcibly removed, thereby telling its tale of violence and maybe robbery and sacrilege. Some examples of this type of chest are:

Essex | Great Burstead, Rayleigh, Stisted, West Hanningfield, and White Notley. All contain money slots and all except Langham and West Hanningfield have three locks. Oak C12.

The West Hanningfield chest is the longest in the county being eight feet one and a half inches long, two feet two inches wide and one foot six and a half inches deep. It is divided into two unequal compartments. The cavity is roughly gouged out and the walls are of great thickness, the ends of each being eight inches and the division ten inches thick. There is a rebate of two inches on which the lid rests which gives a visible thickness of six inches to each end when the chest is closed. The top of the chest is bound with iron on both edges and the edges of each lid are similarly bound. The larger section of the lid, four feet three and a half inches long, has five strap hinges right across the lid, down the back and under the chest to the front, except where they are corroded and broken. The smaller lid, two feet four inches long, has three hinged encircling bands, two of which have partially corroded away. In this lid is a money slot. Each section has a lifting handle of a later date. The middle band on each lid is jointed with a hasp. The left one was for a lock but this has been wrenched out and a staple fixed in the cavity and adapted for a padlock. The one on the right retains an ancient padlock.

The front has two horizontal bands and a curious

fragment of iron which may, perhaps, have been used to cover a flaw in the wood. The irons at the ends have mostly corroded away.

Gloucestershire	Bishop's Cleave, C12.
Hereford and Worcester	Eckington, C12. Elm.
Warwickshire	Curdworth, ten feet long. Iron bound and divided into two compartments. C12. Shustoke, over eight feet long with three locks.

Some of the dug-out chests had coved lids made from portions of tree trunks, as at Little Waltham, Essex, a method which was used later when chests were built of planks, as at Great Tey, Essex, and later still we find both the chest and coved lid completely built of planks, as at High Laver, Essex. The Little Waltham dug-out is excavated in two parts with great skill, the dividing wall being part of the original trunk left by the craftsman. The lid also has been hollowed with an adze. The chest is covered with vertical and horizontal ironwork. An interesting feature is that the uppermost band has been left intentionally higher than the edge of the trunk into which the rebate of the lid falls, thus providing greater security. The three iron bands on the ends turn at the angles onto the front and back. Lifting rings are set through staples at the ends through which chains or ropes could be passed to enable the chest to be slung on a pole for carrying. Each section of the lid is bound round the lower edge with iron, the longer section, three feet seven and a half inches long, has hasps for one lock and two padlocks and the smaller two feet seven inches has the same number of fastenings.

In the thirteenth century chests were constructed on a different principle embodying two features peculiar to the age. One was the use of very broad stiles or standards to the front and back of the chest and the other was the working of the lid on a pin or pivot hinge.

This type of chest was introduced during the time of the papal decree of Innocent III and so accounts for the money slot existing in some of them as, for example, Heckfield, Hampshire, but the majority have no such provision. This is explained by the decrees of English prelates in 1287 and 1289. The reason for which chests were originally provided no longer stirred the country to its former enthusiasm and the money slot is not found in the majority of the chests of this and succeeding centuries as they were, by inference, forbidden as perverting ecclesiastical customs. The manufacture of chests for the purpose of the Crusades was ended but they were now to be made for another reason, ordered by a local Synod but which was not, however, limited to one diocese and prevailed for centuries throughout the English Church.

The Synod of Exeter, 1287, presided over by Bishop Quivil, declared that every parish church should provide, 'cistam ad libros et vestimenta', that is, 'box for the purpose of books and clothes', used in church services.

Bishop Quivil, however, condemned the use of a box, either in or outside the church, in which alms should be dropped as it led to argument between the rector and his parishioners as some people declared that it was better that money should be put into the common box rather than to give it to the priest. In this way the priests failed to get their customary offerings, e.g. donations towards the candles on the Feast of the Purification and other festivals as the money went into the hands of the wardens for lighting the great Crucifix etc. The bishop consequently ordered such chests to be removed from churches and cemeteries in his diocese.

Gilbert, Bishop of Chichester, was not in favour of anything which diverted the alms of the faithful from their canonical course and in 1289, two years after Bishop Quivil's orders, he decreed, 'That hereafter no hollow trunks shall be erected in the parish churches of our diocese, as has been hitherto done by the simplicity and convenience of the parochial clergy, since the parishioners maliciously and damnably put into these trunks the oblations which were wont to be offered to those who minister to God at the altar.'

It would appear from these two decrees that it may be concluded that no more trunks or chests with money slots were made and that from then on chests would be made to contain books and vestments.

Chest development in the thirteenth century was brought about by the art of joinery which resulted in boarded or planked chests. These chests were made of large planks back and front which were nailed with wrought iron nails onto the two ends, strongly clamped and bound with iron. The bottom was grooved and nailed in. There were many varieties of chests during this period and the new technique of boarded chests was a great improvement on the dug-out as it allowed for much larger cavities in deeper and wider chests which did not have to be so long as the dug-outs. Another type is to be found in the construction of the chest at Little Canfield, Essex, which is an exceptionally fine specimen and probably one of the best of its kind to be found in England. It has broad stiles, formed of slabs of oak, which extend below the body of the chest. Into these other slabs of oak are mortised to form the wall of the chest. The front slabs are frequently in one piece as at Little Canfield and Eastwood, Essex, but occasionally they may be of two or more boards laid horizontally as at Pagglesham, Essex, where there are two boards and at Wennington, Essex, where there are three boards. Sometimes

LITTLE CANFIELD, ESSEX.
Stiled chest C13.

the stiles are cut even with the bottom of the chest like the one at Pagglesham, but originally the stiles extended below the body of the chest to provide legs which raised it above the damp flooring of the church. It is very probable that the bottoms of the stiles rotted and had to be removed.

Decoration of the woodwork began to come in and this may be seen on the Little Canfield chest where the stiles on the front are each pierced on the inner side in a semicircle with a chamfered edge, leaving a delicate shaft with disc terminals across the chord of the arc and a disc midway within the curve. Similar feet are to be found elsewhere, e.g. Westminster Abbey and Chichester Cathedral. The rails which are pin-hinged, are fastened to the lid by nails and there are three hasps fastened on the inner side of the lid which fall over staples and are secured with padlocks. The pin hinge was constructed by fastening a rail to each end of the lid by wooden pegs. The back and end of each rail is cut into a half joint and the tops of the back stiles into slots and rounded to give play to the lid. The half-joints of the rails are fitted into the slots and through the stiles and the rails a wooden peg is driven horizontally and is kept from working out by a small plate of iron.

The absence of true hinges rendered the back part of the chest vulnerable

Pin hinge.

to leverage and to guard against this the chests were sometimes strengthened by small chains fastened to staples driven through the back and attached to iron bands that crossed the lid (Climping, W. Sussex and Hatfield Peverel, Essex). The front and back slabs are fastened in position in mortices in the stiles which are cut perpendicularly the whole depth of the front. Some chests, usually on the left side, have a small 'trough' or 'purse' fixed across the end. Chests with this kind of pivot hinge continued to be made occasionally until the fifteenth century.

The early joinery was often not strong enough to give sufficient security so ironwork was again used to hold it all together and to restrict warping which would destroy the shape. Chests, more or less covered by iron straps are found of all ages but the use of ironwork became more apparent in the thirteenth century. In 1220 the relics of St Thomas of Canterbury (Becket) were enclosed in a chest studded with iron nails and secured with iron locks.

The chest at Whittlesford, Cambridgeshire, is eight feet long and is held together by a mass of iron bands running vertically and horizontally and having five locks. The weight of this chest must be enormous and in fact the lid is so heavy that two handles are fixed to the top and it takes two men, standing at the back, to lift it.

The demand for chests resulting from the various orders must have been considerable because by the thirteenth century the making of chests and coffers had become a recognised industry, or 'mistery' (derived from the French 'mestire', a trade) and the manufacturers were themselves incorporated as a Guild. The craft of Cofferers is included in a list of the misteries drawn up in 1328 and the Guild of Cofferers in a list of Craft Guilds in the year 1422. In this connection the name 'cofferer' was also a name given to the person in a large household responsible for the handling of money, usually the steward or chamberlain, which was kept in a coffer. In other words he was a treasurer.

Many parish churches had a large number of vestments while a cathedral or abbey church had a rich collection. Durham Cathedral, in addition to six

BRECON, WALES, ST JOHN (CATHEDRAL).
Quadrant panelled cope chest.

SALISBURY CATHEDRAL, WILTSHIRE.
Late C13 semicircular cope chest. Chip carving.

almeries and a press full of vestments, had eleven chests devoted to vestments. In cathedrals, abbeys and other large churches receptacles, other than chests, were often provided for the careful keeping of vestments but they were also specially designed to accommodate copes which were semicircular capes of rich material fastened with a metal or embroidered clasp (a 'morse') and decorated with a hood and embroidered bands ('orphrey'). The chest was, therefore, constructed in the form of a quadrant in which the cope, folded once, is quadrant, like the fourth segment of a circle and could be kept without undue creasing.

Some fine cope chests may be seen at Brecon Cathedral, Wales; Salisbury Cathedral, Wiltshire and York Minster where there are two, one of the twelfth century and another of the thirteenth century made of oak with leather-covered top and sides.

Ornamentation may now be found in the form of roundels, called chip carving. These roundels contain geometrical patterns executed by a carpenter with a knife or chisel, and continued to be used as decoration into the Jacobean period where they may be found on pulpits but they are much shallower and more delicate. Good examples of chip carving may be seen at St John's, Glastonbury, Somerset and Chichester Cathedral, Sussex. Towards the end of the thirteenth century chip carving developed beyond the roundels and became arcading, following the same designs as the wooden screens and stone window

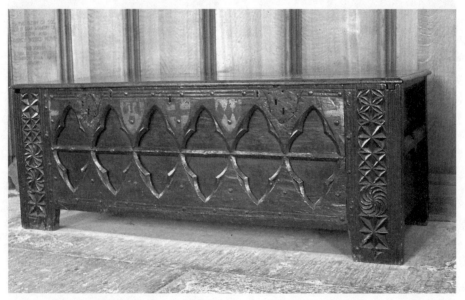

GLASTONBURY, SOMERSET (ST JOHN).
Late C13 chest. Chip carving.

tracery. At Climping, West Sussex, is a fine thirteenth-century chest with roundels of rosette design on the stiles and pointed trefoiled arcade work on the centre panel. This chest has a money slot. It is often stated that the money slots in early church chests and boxes of various sorts were for the collection of Peter's Pence, which was an annual tribute of one penny from every householder possessed of land of a certain value paid to the Papal See from the reign of King Alfred (871–899) until Henry VIII's break with Rome. It was then discontinued by statute in 1534.

Dr Charles Cox in his book, *English Church Fittings, Furniture & Accessories* sets out reasons as to why this statement is quite erroneous. He explains that this payment was at no time a freewill offering left to the discretion of the faithful. The collectors of this payment were specially appointed officials who collected this due from each householder. It was gathered in fixed sums, on a particular date, throughout every deanery in the kingdom. the money slots, on close examination, almost invariably show traces of having been cut in the lids at a later date than the construction of the chest. Dr Cox concludes that the making of these holes was probably a cheap way of complying with the general order of the sixteenth century for the provision of a Poor Man's Box ordered by an Act of Edward VI, 1552. This Act directed that the parishioners in every parish should provide a strong chest with a hole in the upper part and having three keys, to be used for holding alms for the poor. This Act was repeated in the reign of Elizabeth I and reinforced in the canons of 1603. It is doubtful whether this duty would have been committed to the comparative insecurity of a parish chest or even to it being dropped in coin by coin. It is more probably that the pre-Reformation money slots were either for contributions to some general parochial fund or perhaps where a chest belonged to a Guild it was used for the monthly, quarterly or occasional payments from its members. The amount collected for the Papal See was comparatively small amounting to some £200 for the whole country.

Before leaving the thirteenth century mention must be made of the chest in Newport, Essex, which is probably the finest chest of the period in the country. It is an oak stiled chest but the stiles are not so broad as was usual in the thirteenth century, neither is the lid pin-hinged. The front is divided into three horizontal stages with four bands of iron which are carried completely round the chest, each side being divided into two divisions by a central perpendicular band, all fastened in position by nails with conical heads.

In the top stage are twelve shields carved in relief and having concave surfaces, four of them being damaged by modern keyholes and another cut down almost level with the surrounding wood. Besides the original lock, which is complete, there are four other locks which have been added at some later

NEWPORT, ESSEX.

C13 portable altar chest. Lid forms reredos (Holy rood and saints). Compartment for sacred vessels, pax, vestments, missal and reliquaries. A board was probably used as a mensa on which to place a super altar.

Drawing of Newport chest interior.

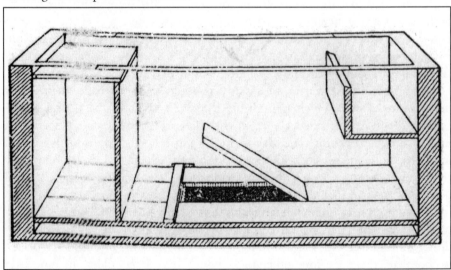

date. The concave surfaces of the shields rather discountenances the theory that they were at one time painted with armorial charges. It would seem that they were, originally, covered by some object, possibly metal escutcheons which were painted with coat armour. If these shields had been left untouched they would, no doubt, have provided some information about the history of this magnificent chest and its family connections.

The middle stage of the front has a band of open tracery cast in lead, gilded and fitted into lozenge-shaped compartments which are divided by narrow rounded ridges in wood. The lead work is not original but has been copied from a small section of the old lead work which survived. It is said that this original fragment is in the Victoria and Albert Museum. The bottom stage contains twelve circular sunken panels with chamfered edges.

The one lock-plate is in the centre of the upper stage and has slightly curved edges with a protruding rim to receive the skeleton hasp while the keyhole is covered by a narrow movable piece of iron. The plate is held in position with large chiselled headed nails. At the centre front and back and at each end are plain drop handles to enable the chest to be lifted.

Perhaps the most interesting feature of this chest is the lid which is encased in a massive frame which has been renewed at some period. This frame extends some four inches over the edges of the actual lid on the top and internally forms the framing of five panels each of which contains a painting. Each panel contains an oil painting of a figure within a trefoil headed arch. In the middle is the Crucifixion with St Mary on the right of the Saviour and St John the Divine on the left. To the right of the Blessed Virgin is St Peter and to the left of St John is St Paul. The figures and architecture are painted in flat tints of black, indigo, blue, vermilion, white and crimson, with a greenish-yellow on the shafts. Mr Roe in his book, *Ancient Coffers and Cupboards*, says, 'The painting of the Newport coffer proves exclusively that oil was used as a vehicle in England at this early period. It may be regarded as the earliest national specimen of that art remaining.'

There would seem to be no doubt that this chest was fitted up as a portable altar for a wealthy official on foreign service. A similar chest is known to have belonged to the Earl of Northumberland in 1513 which was a portable altar carried with him on his military expeditions. It is described as, 'a coffer with two lids, to serve for an altar if need be, the over lid painted with a Crucifix, Mary and John, a super-altar, cloth and vestment and all other stuff to be put in the said coffer'. This is a very similar description to the Newport chest except that the Essex chest is missing the second lid or mensa. There are no indications that a second lid was ever hinged on to the chest but the mensa was probably a board that could rest on the top of the locker and 'purse' as there is at the present time. The chest, internally, has a false bottom with a trap door in the centre plank and having a sliding bar covering the lip. This secret locker would have contained the super-altar which, as already noted, was a small thin piece of stone approximately ten inches by eight inches and three-quarters of an inch thick which had been consecrated by the bishop. This altar-stone would have been placed on top of the wooden mensa so ensuring that the celebration of Mass was lawful.

On the right-hand side, near the top, is an open trough or 'purse', seven and a half inches wide and five and a half inches deep and on the left-hand side is a locker one foot two inches wide which goes down to the false bottom. The lid of this locker works on a pin hinge and is decorated with beading.

The use of ironwork found on thirteenth century chests continued into the sixteenth century. Many of them were so covered in iron that they were 'armour plated'. The methods of locking also varied considerably and some of the locking bars on the insides and outsides of chests, operated by keys, were very intricate. Examples may be seen at Little Bentley, Essex and Sawley, Derbyshire.

The fourteenth century chests had narrower stiles and the legs are frequently made by extending the end planks on each side and cutting V shapes out of

BRENT KNOLL, SOMERSET.
C14 chest with iron bands having fleur-de-lis finials. Padlocks believed to be original.

DEBDEN, NR. NEWPORT, ESSEX.
C14 chest 7ft 10in long with three long hasps and two lifting rings at each end.

the bottom edges to form the four legs. Many of these earlier chests were strengthened, especially during time of trouble, for example during the discontent caused by the Poll Tax in 1381. One object of the rebels was to destroy the rolls on which the services due by the peasants were recorded. These rolls were usually kept in chests either in the manor house or deposited in the church. Copford, Essex, has a fine fourteenth century chest heavily strengthened. This chest is in two compartments with the lid made accordingly. Each section of the lid is bound with iron around the edges with bands across the width corresponding in number and position to those on the front, each of them forming a hinge. The lids, when closed, come within the iron-framed edge of the chest over which fold the hasps of five locks, two for the smaller lid and three for the larger. There are indications that there were originally a greater number of locks securing the larger lid. Three hasps fall over staples for fastening with padlocks and two have lock plates contemporary with the chest. There is also a money slot which has subsequently been made in the smaller lid.

One of the best made and perfectly preserved chests of this period in probably the whole country is at St Mary the Virgin and All Saints, Debden, Nr. Newport, Essex. It was, at some time in the past, painted white and it may be partly due to this that it is in such good condition. The chest is made of oak and very strongly cross-bound with iron. Three long hasps are secured over staples for padlocks. The middle one is larger than the others and reaches almost to the floor. At the end of the hasp is a ring to raise it and at the upper part there is a piece of iron curving outward to assist leverage in raising the large and very heavy lid. The length of this chest is seven feet ten inches, width two feet and depth two feet five inches.

On the inside of the front are two large bolts each of which is shot through six heavy staples fixed in the lid, the bolts being worked from the top of the lid in which there are two keyholes. The inside is divided into two compartments, the smaller one probably being used as a receptacle for chalices, patens, service books, etc. The larger compartment would have been for vestments and altar cloths. There are two lifting rings at each end of the chest. Icklingham, All Saints, Suffolk, has a magnificent early fourteenth century chest which is covered with beautiful wrought ironwork which must be some of the finest in existence. The pattern is formed of almost one hundred scrolls finished with stamped tendril ornament.

During the fourteenth century chests were frequently decorated with carving usually composed of chip carving in the form of roundels as well as tracery,

GREAT TEY, ESSEX.
C17 iron coffer – Flemish. Rests on heavy axles of 4 iron wheels of two sizes. Painted panels, probably a dower chest later presented to the church.

GREET TEY, ESSEX.
C17 iron coffer showing intricate lock mechanism covering inside of lid.

quatrefoils etc. Good examples may be seen at Broxbourne, Hertfordshire; Faversham, Our Lady of Charity, Kent and Rainham, Essex. Some of the finest examples are of Flemish work although much of the work was possibly done in England by English craftsmen using Flemish designs. The Flemings, following political and industrial upheaval, took up residence in East Anglia and there are some fine examples of these carved chests, also chests of iron, to be seen. It is to the Flemings' wealth and piety that we are indebted for the rebuilding of many churches and the foundation of numerous chantries, for the flush work art, their carvings in wood and refined metalwork. The Flemish chest at Chevington, Suffolk, has some fine tracery and carvings of birds, a winged monster and apes shaking hands. Crediton, Devon, also has a splendid chest constructed by Flemish or Dutch craftsmen which has five arches, a wonderful lock with flowers in the corners and a panel showing the Wise Men paying homage with Mary and Joseph among the oxen and two angels kneeling by the Child.

The Flemish craftsmen also made chests of iron and a fine specimen is in Great Tey church, Essex. It is three feet two inches in length, one foot seven and a half inches in width and one foot eight and a half inches in depth with wheels which add a further three and a half inches to the depth. It is strongly banded and riveted, the banding forming panels which are painted. The lid projects slightly over the sides of the chest which rests on the heavy axles of four iron wheels of two sizes unequally spaced and there is an iron drop handle at each end to help guide the chest when being moved. There is an intricate system of security. In the centre of the lid, which closes with a spring, is a disc which turns on a pivot exposing a keyhole. The key moves a lock which covers the inside of the lid, withdrawing nine bolts sprung into the surrounding sides. On the front are two irons fastened by ring staples into the crossed bands. The two irons close upwards over projecting hasps and other staples for padlocks. These have to be removed before the unlocked lid can be raised. A very intricate security system. The exterior panels are painted in muted colours with a man in courtly dress and a woman in a wheel-farthingale and petticoat; foliage and bursting pomegranates. In the centre front is a four-pointed star-like ornament of iron in convex relief gilded and having black veins.

It is said that this chest originally contained the trousseau of a Dutch bride but is more probably a money or dower chest which was later presented to the church.

As already mentioned the Flemings were noted for their refined metalwork which is apparent in many of the lock plates to be found on their chests. A

EAST DEREHAM, NORFOLK.
C16 Flemish chest. Very fine with panelling and beautiful lock plate. Chest not originally intended for a church.

FINGRINGHOE, ESSEX.
Dug-out chest with coved lid. Nail decoration later. The ends of the baulk of timber show the tree ring growth patterns.

fine example is the chest, *c.*1500, to be seen at East Dereham, Norfolk, which has an exquisite lock plate which is earlier than the chest.

With the rise of the guilds and the increase of chantries the number of altars in churches greatly increased and so many more chests were required. The great demand for these resulted in their manufacture becoming a recognised industry.

Most of the guild chests were bought by the fraternity but occasionally they were received as gifts. In the case of a chantry the founder usually provided all that was necessary for the altars but sometimes other people bequeathed chests to the guilds. Richard Brereley, Rector of Kirk Smeaton, North Yorkshire, in his will of 1507 bequeathed to the chantry at Branburgh his long iron-bound chest in which to keep the chalice, vestments and deeds belonging to the chantry. In following periods many of the older chests which were flat on the ground were beginning to show signs of contact with the damp floors of the churches and so were often given feet, either of wood or of iron. Stansfield, Suffolk, has an early fourteenth century chest to which wooden feet were added in the seventeenth century. The chest at Boston, Lincolnshire, has had supports fitted to raise it off the ground. The coved dug-out chest at

Fingringhoe, Essex has added wooden feet. This chest is decorated with nail heads and on the lid; nail heads form the date 1684 which is evidently the date when the decoration was added. The fine iron-bound sixteenth century chest in Cheshunt church, Hertfordshire, is elevated on four small iron feet, slightly splayed, about three and a half inches in height.

By the fifteenth century stiles had narrowed into a frame with panels between. These early framed chests were just as elaborately carved as the stiled chests. The development can be traced through the fourteenth century with the planked chests with stiles which were still being made. Most of the panelled chests to be found are early sixteenth century but, as already mentioned, a good early fifteenth century example may be seen at St John, Glastonbury, Somerset.

During this period the carving on chests became more elaborate and in York Minster is a very fine Flemish chest of the early fifteenth century with crisp carving of the story of St George and the Dragon with a beautiful princess and showing a relief of a medieval town in the background together with the heads of the king and queen watching from the upper windows of a castle tower.

At the end of the fifteenth century chests with an entirely new type of carving appeared. This was known as 'linenfold' because it resembled pleated cloth, although it had nothing to do with chests for the storage of linen. Examples are to be seen at Hempstead, Norfolk; Thaxted, Essex, and North Cerney, Gloucestershire.

The art of the smith had now attained a position which was almost unrivalled. Much of the ironwork on chests was enriched with flowing scrolls and curves made by moulding irons. The iron straps, lock plates and handle plates were decorated by the smith mainly as the result of using discs of steel or hardened

GLASTONBURY,
SOMERSET.
C15 panelled chest.

iron. Each enrichment had to be struck while red hot on to the appropriate die which demanded exceptional skill to produce accurate results. There were many and various forms of decorative ironwork used by the smith on church chests, such as tendrils with leaf ends, waterleaf, fish tails, twists, etc. which demonstrate the art and skill of the smith whose trade ran through a whole gamut of subdivisions ranging from sheer utility, for example a hook and band for a gate, up to fine art.

Ironwork on chests continued through into the sixteenth century and it is worth examining the various methods of locking church chests and the safeguards used to prevent the lid being forced open. At Hessett, Suffolk, is a chestnut chest where the keyhole is masked by a dummy hasp secured by a bolt and at Stonham Aspall, Suffolk is a huge iron-bound chest eight feet long and thirty-one inches wide which is fastened by a bar and eight locks.

Plain panelled chests were common throughout the sixteenth century. It would seem that the modern form of dovetailing was attempted but did not become popular until the seventeenth and eighteenth centuries. An early effort may be seen at North Shoebury, Essex, but it would appear to have been beyond the joiner's powers as it was not continued throughout the work. A seventeenth century specimen may be seen at Tollesbury, Essex, where the ends and sides are neatly dovetailed together.

The iron straps on sixteenth century chests are not usually of the same thickness as formerly and it became the custom to have a chest for commercial affairs and another made purposely for documents which was often covered with leather and iron bound. Examples of these leather-covered chests may be seen at West Mersea and Rainham, Essex.

In the early seventeenth century, following the stripping of our churches in the reign of Edward VI, church chests lost their use and there are instances of their sale being recorded. In the majority of cases it would only have been the least attractive and cheapest kind of chest that was retained for the parish registers and documents. Strong chests were no longer required for rich vestments or valuable chalices, the king had taken them! No longer were chests made to serve the use of a poor box, receptacles were provided for this purpose, but they were required for the preservation of documents.

As a result of the upheavals under the name of religion there was, apart from the loss of service books, the loss of family deeds and legal documents and this caused chaos to take place. Title deeds of properties were lost and the more influential but unprincipled characters seized the lands of lawful owners. Indentures were lost and without the indented copy for support agreements were broken by the person who stood to gain the most. Many a man could not legally prove his own identity in the absence of the carefully kept monastic

THAME, OXFORDSHIRE.
Early C17 chest with chip carving.

records and the destruction of notes made on the covers and fly-leaves of old service books as well as other papers formerly kept by the parish priest.

Such a chaotic state could not be allowed to continue so the Vicar-General, Cromwell, Secretary to Henry VIII, in 1538 issued a Royal Injunction directing every incumbent to keep a Register in which he was to enter every Sunday a written record of the weddings, christenings and burials of the preceding week. The keeping and preservation of Registers was again commanded by Royal Injunctions of Edward VI, 1547, and Elizabeth, 1603 and so chests, for this purpose and for commercial documents, were provided by churchwardens. Canon 70 of 1603 commanded the clergy of every parish to keep a Register,

> And for the safe keeping of the said book the Churchwardens, at the charge of the parish, shall provide one sure coffer with three locks and keys; whereof the one to remain with the Minister and the other two with the Churchwardens severally; so that neither the Minister without the two Churchwardens nor the Churchwardens without the Minister shall at any time take that book out of the said coffer.

By about 1600 the plainness of some panelled chests was relieved by inlaying

216

different woods. This developed into a style termed, Jacobean. It is very distinctive as it looks solid and heavy and is frequently black in colour. Chip carving was reintroduced but was inferior and in lower relief than that of the fourteenth century.

The Renaissance influence showed itself in arcading of round-headed arches on the front of chests. It is very common and with other carving looks quite attractive. A good example is at Finchingfield, Essex. Chests became more ornate and the characteristic ornaments disappeared to be replaced by classical or semi-classical details including such unsuitable ornaments as cherubs. The very beautiful chest at Croscombe, Somerset, is completely covered with a design of rosettes and interlacing bands in low relief.

As the seventeenth century advanced design became more constrained and the first part of the eighteenth century saw the beginning of dignity and sensibility. Towards the end of the century walnut became popular as being a comparatively softer wood than oak and it lent itself to the elaborate carving of the period. Oak, however, still continued to be used as did the traditional methods of construction away from urban areas. After the middle of the eighteenth century there are few chests which may be considered as works of art; they were now utilitarian, the need being for a plain, strong box which would provide space for the masses of poor-law papers which began to accumulate and not for a delightful piece of furniture which would adorn the

FINCHINGFIELD, ESSEX.
C17 chest showing Renaissance influence in arcading of round arches.

REEDHAM, NORFOLK.
C18 (1720) deal chest.

church. Some of these chests were made of deal. An example of a deal chest is in Thaxted, Essex, dated 1789 and is known as the 'Yardley Chest' and another at Reedham, Norfolk dated 1720.

Enclosure of land by agreement had been quite usual since the fifteenth century but the wholesale enclosure which took place in the sixteenth century was one of the principal grievances of the rebels who revolted under Kit in 1549. Steps were taken in the reign of Charles I to curb the growth of enclosure in the seventeenth century. In the first half of the eighteenth century there were great changes in agriculture which altered the general public's attitude to land enclosure. These were the introduction of roots as a field crop and the advantage to be obtained by subsoil drainage. Enclosure by private agreement was a long and painful process and so from about 1760 the normal method was by private act of Parliament. The enormous expense attaching to enclosure by parliamentary means caused a demand for a general act to simplify procedure and so the General Enclosure Act of 1801 was enacted. Further acts were passed in 1836 and 1845 which set up a body of Enclosure Commissioners who had authority to sanction the enclosure of land by provisional order and enclosure award. These acts invariably provided that the original award together

CAWSTON, NORFOLK.
C15 oak alms box on
octagon shaft with 3
locks. Having a
pivotted inverted metal
saucer anti-theft device.

with the map or plan, after execution and proclamation, should be deposited in the parish chest, a copy being deposited with the Clerk of the Peace for the county.

Notwithstanding all the various regulations many clergy failed in their duty and so in 1812 in the reign of George III another act was passed, 'for the better regulating and preserving parish and other registers', which were to be kept in iron chests. This was the last regulation regarding church chests as they began to be no longer required as places of safe keeping, their place being taken by steel safes for the keeping of money and communion vessels, and cupboards, which proved more useful for the keeping of prayer and hymn

LUDHAM, NORFOLK.
C15 Large iron-bound
alms box with three
locks.

books, offertory bags, registers, vestments, pulpit or lenten falls, altar frontals and cloths, etc.

In addition to church chests there were also alms boxes, dole cupboards and banner stave lockers to be seen in our old churches.

Alms Boxes: Poor Boxes

Alms boxes or poor boxes have been used at various times during the past eight hundred years to receive the offerings of the people. As has been noted coffers were provided for the receipt of offerings from the faithful in support of the

Crusades. There were also opportunities in many churches for the devout to contribute for blessings received at the shrines of the saints such as St Cuthbert, Durham Cathedral; St Thomas Cantelupe, Hereford Cathedral; and St Wite, Whitchurch Canonicorum, Dorset (near Lyme Regis). There are, however, few pre-Reformation alms boxes left in our churches and none is older than the fifteenth century. Of these there is a tall example at Blythburgh, Suffolk, comprising three traceried panels in front and constructed to stand against a wall. The date is *c.*1475 when the church was rebuilt. The poor box at Kedington, Suffolk is an upright log, hollowed out and roughly shaped into an octagon, the lower part of which is buried in the floor of the nave. It is well secured with iron bands. Runwell, Essex, also has a dug-out alms box of early fifteenth century date.

Other alms boxes of the late fifteenth century and early sixteenth century may be seen at Cawston, Norfolk, where the box is constructed from a hollowed-out block of wood clad in metal and secured with three locks. Further protection is secured internally by a pivotted inverted metal saucer which prevented the money being taken out by means of an instrument passed through the holes in the top. Ludham, Norfolk, also has an alms box constructed from a hollowed-out block of wood as does Selby, North Yorkshire. The poor box at Lodden, Norfolk is unusual as it possesses two boxes side by side, one of which has a money slot. When the sum was collected it was taken out and placed in the adjoining box in the presence of the two churchwardens. The box thus served as a collecting box and a savings bank!

After the suppression of the monasteries the relief which was normally provided to the poor and needy came to an abrupt end and it therefore became a pressing necessity to provide some other help. During the reigns of Edward VI and Elizabeth I the parishioners were asked to help as generously as possible. Sometimes the old chest was used as an alms box but usually a solid well-padlocked box was installed. There are examples of the Elizabethan period to be found at Dovercourt (dated 1589), Felsted, Essex and Bramford, Suffolk, above which on the south-west pier of the nave arcade, incised and coloured is, 'Remember ye poore the scripture doeth record which to them is given is lent unto the Lord, 1591'. It may be that this alms box is a copy of the original. Also Hargrave, Northamptonshire, dated 1597.

Alms boxes of the seventeenth century are fairly numerous and often bear the words, 'Remember the poor'. A good example is at Giggleswick, North Yorkshire, where the box is fixed to a pier and dated 1684. There are a number of boxes which are carved or painted with figures of beggars or cripples. The one at Watton, Norfolk, has the carved figure of a smiling and bearded man holding his hand to receive alms, the money slot being situate just above the hand and lettered, 'Remember the poore, 1639'. At Bedale, North Yorkshire, there is a solid oak pillar, hollowed out and secured with three massive padlocks and at Lostwithiel, Cornwall is an oak alms box of 1645 in the shape of a standing figure with a shield. Tunworth, Hampshire has a square box carved on two sides with two quaint faces with open lips which serve as money slots, one figure has his tongue out perhaps to show his displeasure at the amount of the donation! Pinhoe, Devon, has a well-carved beggar in high relief. He is shown as a sturdy man particularly well dressed holding what looks like a book on the cover of which is carved, 'Ye Poor Man of Pinhoe, 1700'.

Many of the eighteenth century churches in London have more or less elaborate examples of poor boxes and well-designed examples may be seen at St Mary Abchurch, London, EC4, between Cannon Street and King William Street. They are square in form on square pedestals, one on each side of the west vestry door.

In Poynings church, West Sussex, is an alms box dated 1760 standing on a fluted pedestal two feet two inches high. The oak box is carved with a group composed of Faith, Hope and Charity, with a fourth figure rising from a globe. It is said that this alms box was brought from a convent on the Continent.

Aumbries have been considered separately in this book and so there remain two other forms of cupboard which are to be found.

Dole Cupboards

The first is a 'dole cupboard' which was a receptacle for loaves of bread prior to their distribution among the poor. After the dissolution of the monasteries, travellers and the poor could no longer obtain bread and ale at these establishments and so bread doles were increasingly given out from parish churches. These gifts of bread were made possible by well-to-do citizens either out of generosity or perhaps uneasy consciences. It was always a condition that the recipients should attend church service, after which the distribution was made.

The cupboard was usually well made, shallow with the front fitted with ornamental rails to allow the circulation of air. The size varied but most of them were made to take, on average, about a dozen loaves. St Albans Cathedral, Hertfordshire, has three very fine dole cupboards, one of *c.*1620 and two of the time of Charles II.

Axbridge, Somerset, has a dole cupboard of 1690 which is still used for the dole as may be seen in the photograph. In this case the dole cupboard has glass-fronted panelled doors. Above the cupboard are the date and words, '1690. Spearing's Gift. Four shillings per week in bread to be given to the Second Poor of Axbridge for ever, to be paid out of the South Brent Estate'. The

provision of this dole cupboard was made in accordance with the will of William Spearing, dated 1688. The will provided that the recipients were to attend Morning Service and to be 'poor housekeepers' of the parish who received no relief from the public rates.

Ruislip, Greater London, has a beautifully carved bread cupboard dated 1697, with four shelves, decorated pilasters, large decorated bracket and segmental pediment.

In All Saints church, Hereford, Hereford and Worcester are nicely carved double dole shelves of 1683, with the arms of the donor on the pediment.

Banner Stave Cupboards

The second cupboard is the banner stave cupboard or locker. In the medieval church processions with images and banners took place regularly with elaborate ritual, the various guilds displaying their own banners. These were very splendid and richly worked, but it was not the banners which were kept in the banner stave locker but the banner staves, many of which were probably highly decorated as at Low Ham, Somerset, the shafts of processional crosses (the head of an altar cross was usually made in such a way that it could be mounted on a staff for processional use) and the wooden Lenten cross.

These cupboards or lockers are lofty, narrow recesses in church walls usually towards the west end of the nave. The recesses vary from seven to twelve feet high and between one foot and eighteen inches wide and approximately one foot in depth. Sometimes the aperture extends upwards above the external top and in some instances downwards below the external base. The doors have mostly disappeared but there is an example of an original door at Barnby,

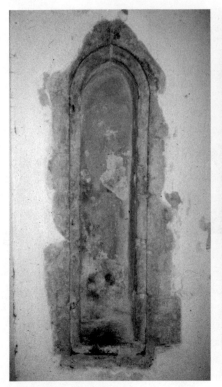

SANDWICH, KENT,
(ST MARY-THE-VIRGIN).
Banner stave cupboard.

CASTLE RISING, NORFOLK.
C14 Banner stave cupboard.

Suffolk. It is six feet eight inches in height, eleven inches wide and one foot in depth. The door is pierced with patterned openings for ventilation purposes. The date is probably fifteenth century and the door has, at some time, been repositioned upside down. The church of St Mary-the-Virgin, Sandwich, Kent also has an original door. Many of the recesses either retain the iron hinges of the original door, or traces where they were fixed, and the grooves for the door. Earls Barton, Northamptonshire has a banner stave cupboard of the fifteenth century with a modern door. Castle Rising, Norfolk, has a fourteenth century cupboard which has a finely carved, cusped and ogee-headed, moulded stone doorway containing a cross and shaft.

It is not understood why most of these cupboards are to be found in East Anglia and Northamptonshire churches.

Examples of chests, alms boxes, dole cupboards, and banner stave cupboards are given below:

Chests

Bishop's Cleeve,	Gloucestershire	C12. Dug-out.
Fownhope,	Hereford & Worcester	C12. Dug-out.
Church Brampton,	Northamptonshire	C13. Good iron scrollwork.
Curdworth,	Warwickshire	C13. Dug-out 10 feet long.
Hindringham,	Norfolk	Very early C13. Stout stiling. Carved with intersecting round arcading.
Stoke d'Abernon,	Surrey	C13. Carved with roundels.
Aldenham,	Hertfordshire	C14. Large chest hollowed out of oak log nine feet eight inches long, clamped with iron. Twelve massive hinges. Sides three feet thick.
Brent Knoll,	Somerset	C14. Ironbound. Two enormous padlocks.
Broxbourne,	Hertfordshire	C14. Carved with Decorated tracery, roundels etc. Length five feet eight inches.
Debden (Nr. Newport),	Essex	C14. Crossbound with iron. Probably one of the best of the period in the country.
Faversham,	Kent	C14. Beautiful front of architectural work.
Pershore Abbey,	Hereford & Worcester	Late C14.
Anstey,	Hertfordshire	C15. Iron-bound.
Blickling,	Norfolk	C15. Iron-bound with five locks. Inscription: 'Mastyr Adam Ilee mad ye Chyst and Robert Filipis payed yerfor God havee marcy on yar soule'.
Brailes,	Warwickshire	C15. Elaborate foliated tracery with Tudor roses.
Southwold,	Suffolk	C15. Beautiful tracery. St George

slaying the dragon portrayed under lock plate.

Baldock,	Hertfordshire	C16. Carved.
Dunmow,	Essex	C16. Beautiful inlaid panels.
Hemel Hempstead,	Hertfordshire	C16. Iron-bound.
Hempstead,	Norfolk	C16. Linenfold panels.
Orsett,	Essex	C16. Good example from reign of Henry VIII in fine state of preservation. Each of four panels decorated with linenfold which is further embellished with two incised crosses and four trefoils. The stile mouldings, brackets, ogee arches at each end and the lock plate are interesting. It is probable that this chest belonged to Edmund Bonner, Bishop of London (1500–1569) who had a palace at Orsett. The chest is rather high from the floor and it is suggested that it may have been used as a credence table in the north chapel.
Southam,	Warwickshire	C16. Large iron-bound with five locks.
Wirksworth,	Derbyshire	C16. panelled chest.
Axbridge,	Somerset	C17. Three painted panels – Betrayal, Charge to Twelve Apostles, Agony in the Garden.
Rickling,	Essex	C17. Three-sided top. Originally covered in leather. Iron-bound, three locks. Fragments of leather where it passes under iron bands. Unusual design of remaining hasp. Lock plates have ornamented strips of iron towards the edges and a

		similar piece is pivoted above the keyhole of each plate to exclude dust.
Baldock,	Hertfordshire	C17. Panelled chest. The four panels are each carved with a capless arch enclosing a lozenge. The framework is ornamented with strap and jewel patterns and on the front on each end and between the panels split pendants are applied.
Bentworth,	Hampshire	C17. Good Jacobean.
Great Clacton,	Essex	C17. Georgian chest with two iron bands at each side the ends turned to the front and terminating in fleur-de-lis. The lid and plinth are moulded and it has three locks.
Theydon Garnon,	Essex	C17. Broad oak slabs with iron bands. Edges of lid and base bound with iron. The spaces between the bands are decorated with nail-heads arranged in double lozenges. On the lid is a plate engraved with the arms of Sir John Archer, Knight with the following inscription: 'The gift of Sir John Archer Knight one of his Ma:ties Judges of the Common-plees. 1668'.
Walcott,	Norfolk	C17. Three sided top. Unusual design.
Black Chapel North End	Essex	C18. Early C18, plain oak chest.
Reedham,	Norfolk	C18. Large panelled chest dated 1790 with names of churchwardens.

Alms boxes

Cawston,	Norfolk	C15.
Blickling,	Norfolk	C17 (1692).

Dovercourt,	Essex	C16.
Halifax,	W. Yorkshire	C17 (1689).
Lostwithiel,	Cornwall	C17 (1645).
Smarden,	Kent	C16 Enamel plate for money–slot. Believed to be Limoges.

Dole cupboards

Axbridge,	Somerset	1690
Milton Ernest,	Bedfordshire	
Hereford,	All Saints Church	
St Albans Cathedral,	Hertfordshire	

Banner stave lockers

Barnby,	Suffolk
Blyford,	Suffolk
Bristol Cathedral,	Avon
Castle Rising,	Norfolk
Cromer,	Norfolk
Earls Barton,	Northamptonshire
Gislingham,	Suffolk
Henstead,	Suffolk
Kelshall,	Hertfordshire
Kingsthorpe,	Northamptonshire
Nuneaton Abbey Church, St Mary,	Warwickshire
Rushmere,	Suffolk
South Cove,	Suffolk
South Walsham,	Norfolk

Bibliography

BAILEY, BRIAN, *Almshouses* (1988).

BOND, FRANCIS, *The Chancel of English Churches* (1916); *Screens and Galleries* (1908); *Misericords* (1910).

BOWYER, JACK, *The Evolution of Church Building* (1977).

BUCKLER, GEORGE, *Twenty-two of the Churches of Essex* (1856).

CAUTLEY, H. MUNRO, *Norfolk Churches* (1949); *Suffolk Churches* (1975); *Royal Arms and Commandments in our Churches* (1954).

COOK, G.H, *Medieval Chantries and Chantry Chapels* (1947).

COX, J. CHARLES, *English Church Fittings, Furniture and Accessories* (1923); *Pulpits, Lecterns and Organs* (1915).

COX, J. CHARLES & HARVEY, ALFRED, *English Church Furniture* (1967).

GARDNER, ARTHUR, *Minor English Wood Sculpture 1400–1550* (1958).

HOWARD, F.E. & CROSSLEY, F.H, *English Church Woodwork* (1927).

KRAUS, DOROTHY & HENRY, *The Hidden World of Misericords* (1976).

LEWER H. WILLIAM & WALL, J. CHARLES, *The Church Chests of Essex* (1913).

PARDOW, ROSEMARY, *Royal Arms in Churches* (Various Counties).

PETCHEY, W.J., *Armorial Bearings of the Sovereigns of England* (1977).

PEVSNER, NIKOLAUS, *The Buildings of England Series* (Various Counties).

PLATT, COLIN, *The Parish Churches of Medieval England* (1981).

RANDALL, GERALD, *Church Furnishing & Decoration in England and Wales* (1980).

ROE, FRED, *Ancient Church Chests and Chairs in the Home Counties round Greater London* (1929).

SUMMERS, PETER & others, *Hatchments in Britain* (Various Counties).

TASKER, EDWARD G, *Encyclopedia of Medieval Church Art* (1993).

VALLANCE, AYMER, *Greater English Church Screens* (1947); *English Church Screens* (1936).

Glossary of Terms

ALMERY. A place for alms. A cupboard.

APSE. Semicircular or polygonal end to a chancel or chapel and sometimes found as a termination to transepts or nave (Langford, Essex).

AUGURIES. The foretelling of events by observing and interpreting signs and omens.

AUMBRY. Small wall recess used as a cupboard.

BULL. An official document issued by the Pope and sealed.

CANONIST. A person skilled in canon law.

CANONS REGULAR. Groups of priests who were members of a religious community and lived under a rule.

CANONS SECULAR. Priests not living under monastic vows or religious community.

CELURE. Section of roof immediately above Rood screen, sometimes richly decorated as a canopy to the Rood.

CHIP CARVING. Simple type of carved ornament used on wooden surfaces. Usually geometrical patterns first set out with compasses and then chipped out.

CIBORIUM. Covered receptacle for storing the consecrated Hosts. Also applied to a canopy over the altar which was usually erected on four pillars and called a baldachino.

COAT ARMOUR. A coat of arms. A 'man of coat armour' is one who bears arms.

CONFESSIO. An underground chamber usually below east end of a church in early medieval times for the burial of martyrs, saints etc., or a cavity in an altar for housing relics.

CONVOCATION. A clerical assembly or synod.

COPE. A semicircular piece of cloth worn around the shoulders and held together at the front by a clasp (morse).

CORBEL. A projecting block of stone or timber to support a feature above.

COVE. A large concave curve supporting the projecting rood loft.

ENCHANTMENT. A magic spell.

FESS POINT. Centre of the shield.

FINIAL. An ornament terminating a pinnacle, gable, canopy etc.

GESSO. Hard fine plaster.

GREEK CROSS. A cross formed by two plain arms of equal length crossing at the middle at right-angles to each other.

230

GUARDANT. With face looking outwards.

HERSE. Framework with sockets for candles or tapers placed over coffin. Permanent herses were later used to place over tombs of distinguished people so that candles could be lighted on the anniversary of their deaths.

HOMILY. A sermon intended to moralise rather than to explain religious doctrine.

INDULGENCE. Remission from purgatory, i.e. punishment from certain sins.

LEGERDEMAIN. Deception or trickery, sleight of hand.

KNOT. Protrusion on stem.

MENSA. Stone altar slab incised with five consecration crosses.

MUNTIN. The vertical part in the framing of a door, screen, panelling, etc.

MURAL. A painting or decoration applied directly to a wall or ceiling, e.g. Fresco: painting onto damp plaster; Secco: painting onto dry plaster – method usually employed in Britain.

NECROMANCY. The art of communing with the spirits of the dead in order to predict the future.

PALL. A cloth cover usually of black or purple velvet used to cover a herse.

PASSANT. Beasts who are walking with dexter forepaw raised.

PISCINA. A water drain in the floor or wall near an altar.

POLYCHROME. Colouring of walls, architectural ornaments, etc. in many and various colours.

PRICKET. A small spike for holding a candle upright.

PYX. Receptacle used to carry the Blessed Sacrament suspended over the High Altar.

RELIQUARY. Container for relics, sometimes in the shape of that part of the body, the fragments of which the reliquary contained.

REREDOS. Enriched screen behind and above an altar.

ROOD. Christ on the Cross flanked by figures of Mary and John.

SACRING BELL. External bell rung during Mass so that people unable to be present at Mass may bow their knees (Archbishop Pecham/Peckham 1281).

SCONCE. Iron Bracket fixed to wall to hold a candle.

SEDILIA. Wall seats on the south side of the sanctuary for the celebrant and other priests at high Mass.

SPANDREL. Triangular space between the side of an arch and its containing rectangle. Also applied to the surface between two arches in an arcade.

STILE. Vertical member in the framing of a door panelling or other woodwork.

TABERNACLE. Canopied structure to contain the Reserved Sacrament or a relic.

TESTER. Flat canopy over a pulpit or altar.

TIPPET. A long streamer which hung from the elbow.

Index of Places

General Index

Abbot, Archbishop, 177, 178
Act of Settlement, 1701, 187
Aelfric, Abbot of Eynsham, Oxfordshire, 105
Alfred, King, 46, 205
Algrand, 152
Alms boxes, 220
Altar, 25, 155
   candlesticks, 147
   Christ's board, 25
   consecration crosses, 25
   coverings, 38
   God's board, 25
   gradine, 30
   position of, 33
   rails, 33, 34
   removal of stone, 31
   reredos, 29
   stone, 25
   super, 15, 16
   wooden, 25
Anglo-Saxon gospels, 133
Annates, 185
Anne, Queen, 177, 185
Arundel Lord of Wardour, 183
Astbroke, Robert, 156
Aumbries, 21

Bancroft, Richard, Archbishop of Canterbury, 31
Banner stave cupboards, 223
Barrow, Isaac, 108
Baxter, Richard, 108
Beadle, Theodore, 179
Beaufort, Cardinal Henry, 162

Bede roll, 151, 152
Bedesmen, 155
Bede, Venerable, 105
Bench-ends, 80
   auxiliary seats, 83
   carving, 86
   finials or 'poppy-heads', 83
Bishop's throne, 68
Bond, Francis, 15, 48
Books, chained, 133
Branches (iron brackets with prickets), 143
Brereley, Richard, Rector, 213
Buckler, George, 48
Bunyan, John, 64
Butler, Nicholas, 183

Camden, William, 175
Candle-beam, 143
Candle-holders, 147
Candlesticks, altar, 147
Canute, King, 151
Caroline Divines, 34
Catlyn, John, 183
Chained books, 133
Chairs, 63
Chantries and chantry chapels, 151
   suppression of, 165
Chantry, foundation of perpetual, 154
Chantry priest, 154, 159, 164
Charities Act, 1547, 166, 168
Charles I, King, 177, 178, 179, 180, 218
Charles II, King, 108, 119, 179, 180, 182, 186, 222
Church chests, 195

Church Commission for England, 186
Civil War, 119
Commonwealth, 178
Commonwealth Parliament, 36
Confessio, 29
Confraters, 151
Cook, G. H., 168
Cope chest, 204
Corbett, Richard, Bishop of Norwich, 93
Cornburgh, Avery, 163
Corona, 143
Cosin, John, 35, 120
Coverdale, Miles, 136
Cranmer, Thomas, Archbishop of Canterbury, 136
Cresset stones, 140
Cromwell, Thomas, 136, 216
Crusades, money for, 196, 221

Dashwood, Sir Francis, 132
Decorated period, piscina, 11
Dissolution of the monasteries, 168
Dole cupboards, 222
Donne, John, 119
Dowsing, William, 34

Earl of Northumberland, 207
Early English period, angle-piscina, 10
Ecclesiastical Commission, 186
Edward I, King, 153
Edward IV, King, 163, 172
Edward VI, King, 31, 107, 108, 116, 136, 166, 167, 173, 215, 221
Edward VI, Act of 1550, 31
Edward VI, Act of 1552, 205
Edward VI, Injunctions 1547, 136, 216
Edward VII, King, 194
Edward VIII, King, 194
Eleanor of Castile, Queen, 153
Elizabeth I, Queen, 108, 116, 221
Elizabeth I, Injunctions 1559, 31, 107, 108
Elizabeth I, Injunctions 1603, 206, 216
Elizabeth II, Queen, 194

Elizabethan Settlement, 116

Ferrer, Nicholas, 35
Flemish chest work, 211, 212, 214
Friars, 106
Fridstool, 66
Fuller, Thomas, 35

Galleries 93
General Enclosure Acts, 1801, 1836, 1845, 218
George I, King, 187, 189
George II, King, 190
George III, King, 188, 189, 191, 219
George IV, King, 191, 192
George V, King, 194
George VI, King, 194
Gilbert, Bishop of Chichester, 200
Gilds, trade, 161
Gradine, 30
Grandison, John, Bishop of Exeter, 129
Grosseteste, Robert, Bishop of Lincoln, 105
Guild chests, 213
Guild of Cofferers, 202

Hagioscopes, 46
Hanbage, Thomas, 178
Harold, King, 151
Hatchments 95
  background, 95
  cadency marks, 97
  motto, 97
Henry II, King, 196, 197, 198
Henry IV, King, 171
Henry VI, King, 163
Henry VII, King, 174
Henry VIII, King, 133, 134, 165, 166, 172, 174, 175, 177, 205
Henry of Blois, Bishop of Winchester, 162
Herbert, George, 108
Hearse, 158
Hour-glasses, 109, 122